GONE BUT NOT FORGO

East Anglia's Lost Double-[

Operators that have disappeared since WWII

Geoff R Mills

Right to left: WH 810, DPU 747, PTW 625
This superb line up in Braintree bus station on 1 August 1950 shows three Hicks Bros double-deckers at rest between duties: 50 (WH 801) a 1928 Leyland TD1 ex Bolton, is ready to work the service to Witham; 49 (DPU 747), a 1936 Leyland TD4/Park Royal new to Hicks and PTW 625, a 1950 Guy Arab III/Strachan which had been ordered by Hicks but delivered after Eastern National took control (hence the livery of green with two cream bands). 49 and 50 are still in Hicks livery of blue with three golden yellow bands, which gradually disappeared in the early 1950s.   *Derek S Giles*

Published by:
M W Transport Publications
12 Saxon Close
Lexden
Colchester
CO3 4LH
01206 766886

ISBN 0952 7770 7 X

GONE BUT NOT FORGOTTEN

East Anglia's Lost Double-Deckers

Contents and list of operators

Introduction

Why just double-deckers? My earliest interest was the observation of Colchester Corporation Transport buses and the entire fleet at that time was double-deck. Visits to the town's bus station in St Johns Street, revealed more double-deckers with operators including Blackwell's, Chambers, Moore's, Norfolk's and Osborne's so it appeared to a novice enthusiast that any substantial bus business had double-deckers as the backbone of the fleet. The seed was sown as my mobility increased with visits to such places as Sudbury and Bury St Edmunds where the variety of double-deckers was manifold.

In the aftermath of World War II, came the freedom to travel, this coupled with the "baby boom" as a result of the troops returning to civilian life after years in the armed services, resulted in the need for large vehicles for school transport. To cover such work, many operators who had hitherto only operated coaches, were encouraged to acquire double-deckers. The problem then arose as to availability as the major operators were desperately awaiting new deliveries before releasing any time expired stock onto the second-hand market. This meant an interesting array of well-used vehicles were acquired by the independents who were eager to meet the demand. In those truly halcyon days when queues formed and reliefs were frequently required, only Hicks of Braintree, Moore's of Kelvedon and Osborne's of Tollesbury bought new double-deckers. In fact, of the 45 operators reviewed, only Pegg at Caston bought a new double-decker in the seventies.

Much has been written and published on railway history, on virtually every closed line detailing the fate of the station buildings and the surrounding properties. Little has been penned on similar lines for the lost independent operators and the sites they occupied. In the main most of the properties have been demolished to give way to housing developments, very few have survived intact. Osborne's garage in Tollesbury is a notable exception, having remained a fully operational bus and coach garage after takeover.

Having lived through the exciting years of diversity into double-deckers by so many independent operators in East Anglia, it has been saddening to see over forty cease. However, hopefully all those enterprises that invested in two or more double-deckers from bases in Essex (excluding those in the Metropolitan Traffic Area and the former County Borough of Southend-on-Sea), Norfolk and Suffolk are posthumously mentioned and/or illustrated as a tribute to the endeavours of so many bus operations that no longer exist.

In conclusion, I must extend thanks to many and numerous operators for their assistance and various fellow enthusiasts particularly Maurice Bateman, Peter Clark, Andrew Coleman, Paul Edwards, Andrew Saunders and John Taylor.

G R Mills - September 2006

Other East Anglian publications still available include:
    City Sightseeing - UK operations 1998 - 2003
    Colchester 1904 - 2004 - From Trams to Arriva, a century of service
    Fowlers of Holbeach Drove - 1947 - 2002 - 55 Years of service
    Norfolk's of Nayland - 1843 - 1991 - 75 years of motorised service
    Whippet of Fenstanton - 1919 - 1999 - 80 years of progress

Further details from
M W Transport Publications, 12 Saxon Close, Lexden, Colchester CO3 4LH (01206 766886)

Ashdown's Luxury Coaches Ltd, Maldon Road, Danbury, Essex

This business was founded in 1925 by F H Ashdown, who traded as Rodney Bus Service, a name derived from the terminal point of his service from Danbury to Little Baddow (The Admiral Rodney Inn). Ashdown's service was acquired by Eastern National on 4 December 1937 and incorporated into their service 1B from Chelmsford to Little Baddow via Danbury.

Operations continued to prosper with both new and second-hand Bedford and Dennis coaches added to the fleet. Post war vehicle scarcity prompted the acquisition of three pre-war heavy-duty chassis (2 Leyland and 1 AEC) specified with new Thurgood ½ cab coachwork. These were joined by six Bedford OBs supplied new, largely for private hire duties, while double-deckers were introduced in 1946 for school contracts.

The psv bus and coach enterprise was relinquished in 1963 in favour of a Ford car and van franchise using the modern garage building set in a quarry type location below a filling station on the main road. On retirement of the Ashdown family the site was again occupied by a commercial company, Hoynors, whose main output was steel trailers. In 1964, however, two ex London Transport private hire RFs were smartly repainted from green and grey into duo-red and white for Osborne's of Tollesbury. The property was cleared after the demise of Hoynors but the housing development built on the site has perpetuated the engineering company's name. The filling station survived various ownerships such that 80years after Ashdown's operations commenced the facility was a Tesco Express site.

Livery: cream and orange

Double-Deckers operated 1946 - 1963

	Reg	Chassis	Body	Seats	New	In	Ex	Out
32	JY 5010	Leyland TD5	Weymann	L24/26R	1935	6/46	Plymouth (92)	3/60
34	DR 9871	Leyland TD2	Leyland	L24/24R	1932	4/47	Plymouth (82)	12/51
35	DR 9859	Leyland TD2	Leyland	L24/24R	1932	5/47	Plymouth (70)	5/50
42	HG 2307	Leyland TD3	Park Royal	L26/26R	1933	4/50	Burnley (62)	4/55
45	CTJ 81	Leyland TD5	Leyland	H30/24R	1938	9/53	Accrington (92)	9/57
46	BBA 546	Leyland TD5	Metro-Cammell	H26/22R	1940	11/53	Salford (221)	3/56
47	GKL 759	Leyland TD7	Leyland	H28/26R	1940	7/57	Maidstone & District (DH1)	7/58
52	FEV 176	Leyland TD5	ECW	L27/28R	1937	5/58	United Counties (570)	3/63
53	JPU 640	Bristol K5G	Duple	L27/28R	1942	5/58	Moores, Kelvedon	3/61
54	JVX 223	Guy Arab II	Strachans	L27/28R	1944	10/58	Moores, Kelvedon	3/61

Note - FEV 176 was new to Eastern National (3707) with a Brush L27/28R body and was rebodied in 1949

JY 5010 (left)
The stalwart of the fleet was the first double-decker owned which survived for nearly 14 years. Ex-Plymouth stock was well received in East Anglia and beyond: AA of Ayr, Alexander, Crosville, Eastern Counties, Eastern National, Hants & Sussex, Lowland Motorways, Premier Travel, Thames Valley and United Counties all had examples. Seen in January 1958 with a generous layer of winter road dirt on the side panels, the bus was by then 23 years old and performed as a psv for a quarter of a century.

G R Mills

JPU 640 (right)
This was a unique vehicle with its original/previous owners Moore Bros of Kelvedon, as it was the only Bristol ever operated. Furthermore the bus was one of the unfrozen buses that were under construction at the outbreak of World War II but subsequently released prior to the full utility specification. Seen at the depot yard in May 1959.

G R Mills

J D Best & Son, Frating Road, Great Bromley, Essex
Vine's Luxury Coaches Ltd, Frating Road, Great Bromley, Essex

J D Best commenced operations in April 1952 with the acquisition of C J W Sage of the same address. Later the same year, the new owner's first addition to the acquired fleet was the first double-decker for use on the daily service from the Great Bromley base via Crockleford to Colchester Bus Station. The business changed hands in February 1960 when R L G Catt and R C Swinn assumed control. Again later the same year they reintroduced a double-decker onto the service, Best's having reduced the working to an AEC coach which was traded in for the larger capacity bus.

In April 1964, the business was sold on yet again when F W Vine of Little Clacton and later at Weeley Heath, moved into the bungalow next door, which also served as the office. Vines Luxury Coaches Ltd was formed the following month. 1972 was a tumultuous year for the company as Frank's son-in-law, Terry Wood, who had control of the company, passed it on to Ray James of Dovercourt. A double-decker had been introduced back on to the stage service after a seven-year lapse but the final owner replaced this with a brand-new grant-aided Bedford YRQ/Willowbrook 002 for most journeys (the first new bus since Sage bought a Bedford OB/Duple in 1945). Operations ceased in October 1973 and, while the service passed initially to Hedingham & District Omnibuses, the vehicles were dispersed and the premises became Crossways commercial vehicle base.

Livery: red and cream (Sage's)
        cream and red (Best's)
        maroon, grey and cream (Vine's)

Double-Deckers operated 1952 - 1972

Reg	Chassis	Body	Seats	New	In	Ex	Out
EOG 270	Leyland TD6c	Metro Cammell	H38/28R	1938	12/52	Birmingham (270)	5/54
ADR 795	Leyland TD5	Weymann	L24/24R	1937	5/54	Plymouth (195)	3/59
DJY 965	Crossley DD42/5	Crossley	L27/26R	1947	10/58	Plymouth (335)	5/59
CAP 230	Bristol K5G	ECW	CO30/26R	1940	10/60	Shangri-La, St Osyth	10/62
JFJ 604	Daimler CVD6	Brush	H30/26R	1948	10/62	Exeter (41)	7/64
ECX 420	AEC Regent III	NCB	L29/26R	1948	4/64	Huddersfield (200)	8/65
YJG 809	AEC Bridgemaster	Park Royal	H42/30F	1962	6/72	East Kent	10/72

Notes:
CAP 230 was new to Brighton, Hove & District (6358)

DJY 965 survived into preservation

EOG 270 (right)
The halcyon days of stage service patronage were met by Best's with a traditional ex-Birmingham bus, seen in December 1953, waiting on Stand 22 in Colchester's St Johns Street bus station alongside the timber waiting room. Evidence of the Queen's Coronation celebrations is still visible above the destination box.

G R Mills

ECX 420 (left)
The smartest double-decker to work on the Great Bromley service was Vines fully repainted example, seen in June 1965 crossing the East Gate Junction level crossing (on the line from London to Clacton-on-Sea and Walton-on-the-Naze). The bus subsequently worked for Silver City Coaches at Harlow, and reappeared at Clacton on private hire still in Vines livery.

G R Mills

B M Brandon, School Green, Blackmore End, Essex

Brian Brandon's initiation into the PSV world came when he was a motorcycle enthusiast working in the stores department of a retailer of the two wheeled transport in Colchester, searching for an elderly coach to convert to carry a set of motorbikes to various events. The vehicle he found was a rare Commer Q4 with a Yeates body with Alec Osborne at Blackmore End. Alec was anxious to retire from coaching and persuaded Brian to buy the business, which included three operational Bedford SB's, in August 1967. Brian changed the fleet colours from red and cream to white and yellow and traded under his own name to avoid confusion with the long established and much larger fleet based at Tollesbury. Throughout the seventies and eighties he introduced a Ford bias to the fleet.

Expansion followed the acquisition of the full sized coaches (two Fords and two Bedfords) of Harry Cook of Braintree in July 1978; he retained his minibuses and garage business which continued to trade. Ten years later operations recommenced under the name Flagfinders and by the new millennium, Steve Cook was running six double-deckers.

Following the death of Brian Sibley (t/a Florida Coaches), Halstead, the only double-decker he owned, an ex-London DMS, was acquired by Brandon's in 1983 and this outlived seven similar models purchased subsequently. Ten years later, Florida Coaches was re-formed by Brian Sibley's widow Carol; and her brother, Patrick Keeble, with a fleet of coaches which includes two double-deckers.

By the nineties the Bova Futura was the favoured choice for coaches with six being taken into stock. Four of these were destroyed in a disastrous fire in October 2002, the source of which was the pair of ex-Eastern National long wheelbase Olympians which were reduced to single deck height. The business never recovered from the setback, despite the use of loaned vehicles, no fresh stock was acquired and the work passed to Fargo Coachlines of Rayne. All PSV activity ceased on Brandon's site in 2004 with only car and light commercial work being conducted on the premises.

Livery: white and yellow with brown bands

Double-Deckers operated 1983 - 2002

Reg	Chassis	Body	Seats	New	In	Ex	Out
KUC 217P	Daimler CRL6	Park Royal	H44/32F	1976	4/83	Florida, Halstead	5/03
SOE 922H	Daimler CRG6LX	Park Royal	H47/33D	1970	9/83	Harwich & Dovercourt Coaches	9/96
THM 707M	Daimler CRG6	MCW	H44/32D	1974	12/84	Cedric, Wivenhoe	10/01
GHV 3N	Daimler CRL6	Park Royal	H44/32D	1975	9/85	London Transport (DM1003)	10/01
GHV 23N	Daimler CRL6	Park Royal	H44/32D	1975	9/85	London Transport (DM1023)	2/02
GHV 97N	Daimler CRL6	Park Royal	H44/32D	1975	9/85	London Transport (DM1097)	10/02
GHV 13N	Daimler CRL6	Park Royal	H44/32D	1975	10/85	London Transport (DM1013)	2/02
GHM 813N	Daimler CRL6	MCW	H44/32D	1974	10/85	London Transport (DM1813)	3/86
MLK 677L	Daimler CRL6	Park Royal	H44/34F	1973	9/87	Wiffen, Finchingfield	10/01
OSR 194R	Bristol VRT/LL3/6LXB	Alexander	H49/34F	1977	8/98	Jackson, Bicknacre	9/99
FGE 441X	Dennis Dominator	Alexander	H45/34F	1982	9/98	Liverpool Motor Services	9/99
B690 BPU	Leyland ONTL11/2R	ECW	H45/28F	1985	9/99	Windmill, Copford	10/02
B696 BPU	Leyland ONTL11/2R	ECW	H45/28F	1985	9/99	Windmill, Copford	10/02

Notes:
MLK 677L, THM 707M and KUC 217P were new to London Transport (DMS677, DM1217, DM1707)
SOE 922H was new to West Midlands PTE (3922)
OSR 194R was new to Tayside (194)

FGE 441X was new to Central SMT (D41)
B690 BPU and B696 BPU were new to Eastern National (4502, 4508), subsequently South Wales (908/9)

MLK 677L and GHV 23N
The favoured double-decker throughout Brandon's operation of the breed was the ex-London Transport, Leyland-engined, Daimler Fleetline, most of which operated in original dual-door configuration. MLK 677L was the last example acquired, a particularly well-kept bus that had been converted to single door by Ensign prior to acquisition by Wiffens, seen here at rest in Braintree bus park between school contract journeys in October 1994.

G R Mills

S Blackwell & Sons, Coggeshall Road, Earls Colne, Essex

Sydney Blackwell was a true pioneer and as a young man served on the North West frontier in World War I. Fascinated with the internal combustion engine, Syd was alert to the potential of ex-WD subsidy chassis that were available after November 1919. Syd had bus bodies built on a variety of these surplus chassis and commenced a Halstead - Earls Colne - Colchester stage service in direct competition with the National Omnibus Company.

In the thirties an express service to London was established from Coggeshall, Earls Colne, Halstead and Braintree. Several new coaches were purchased specifically for this service. From 1936 until the sale of the business, every double-decker that Syd purchased was a second-hand Leyland, such that every model from the TD1 to TD5 was operated plus a wide variety of similar vintage saloons in the TS1 - TS8 range, again all pre-owned. The love of the Leyland marque endured and other East Anglian operators were supplied with complete vehicles including Honeywood, Stanstead; Goldsmith, Sicklesmere; Letch, Sible Hedingham; Norfolk, Nayland; Osborne's, Tollesbury; Partridge, Hadleigh and Sage/Best, Great Bromley. In addition Blackwell's undertook heavy mechanical work and supplied parts from the numerous ex-psv stock they dismantled.

The London service had been incorporated into Mulley's (ex Corona) service in 1960 long before the takeover by Hedingham & District Omnibuses in October 1965. Part of the premises was used by Hedingham Omnibuses until vacated in 1971 when the entire yard and adjoining house were sold; the premises becoming C J Services, a commercial vehicle enterprise.

Livery: deep maroon with cream band

Double-Deckers operated 1946 - 1965

Reg	Chassis	Body	Seats	New	In	Ex	Out
UF 5651	Leyland TD1	Leyland	L24/24R	1930	5/38	Southdown (851)	6/50
UF 5538	Leyland TD1	Leyland	L24/24R	1929	8/43	Morley, West Row	4/46
TH 2300	Leyland TD2	Leyland	L24/24R	1932	8/45	J James, Ammanford (29)	3/50
JY 3648	Leyland TD3	Leyland	L24/24R	1934	7/46	Plymouth (15)	6/51
HL 5335	Leyland TD2	Brush	L27/26R	1932	3/50	West Riding (30)	9/56
CWR 282	Leyland TD5	Leyland	L27/26R	1937	6/50	Todmorden (4)	7/56
BEL 391	Leyland TD4	Brush	L27/26R	1935	5/51	Hants & Dorset (995)	8/57
NV 5141	Leyland TD4	ECOC	L30/26R	1935	3/56	Baxter, Hanley	3/58
FEV 182	Leyland TD5	ECW	L27/28R	1937	6/57	United Counties (576)	4/64
FEV 180	Leyland TD5	ECW	L27/28R	1937	12/57	United Counties (574)	10/63
EUH 973	Leyland PD2/3	Leyland	L27/26R	1950	11/63	Western Welsh (973)	10/65
EUH 961	Leyland PD2/3	Leyland	L27/26R	1950	12/63	Western Welsh (961)	10/65

Notes:
UF 5538 was new to Southdown (838)
HL 5335 was new with a Roe H26/22D body
NV 5141 was new to United Counties (410)

FEV 182 was new to Eastern National (3713), later United Counties (576)
FEV 180/182 were new to Eastern National (3711/3) with Brush L27/28R bodies and were rebodied in 1949

Double-Deckers owned in dealer capacity for dismantling 1955 - 1965

Reg	Chassis	Body	Seats	New	Ex
GJ 2011	AEC Regent	Tilling	O33/26R	1930	Eastern National (1008)
CGJ 156	AEC Regent	LPTB	H30/26R	1936	London Transport (STL1158)
DDK 113	Leyland TD5c	Cravens	H28/26R	1938	Rochdale (143)
JTW 749	Guy Arab I 5LW	Park Royal	H30/26R	1943	Colchester (37)
JTW 983	Guy Arab II 5LW	Weymann	H30/26R	1943	Colchester (40)
FEV 178	(Leyland TD5)	Brush	L27/28R	1937	Eastern National (3709)
BDR 262	Leyland TD5c	Weymann	L24/24R	1937	Plymouth (225)

Notes:
GJ 2011 was new to Brighton, Hove & District (6011)
FEV 178 only the body of this vehicle was acquired
BDR 262 was rebodied with a Thurgood C39F body before entering service with Blackwell

JY 3648 (left)
The only Leyland TD3 operated by Blackwell's superseded a Leyland TD1 that was 5 years older but the style of Leyland bodywork suggested a greater time span. All traces of the piano-style front had been eliminated as shown in this St Johns Street bus station, Colchester, view of the TD3 about to take up position on the Halstead stand. The black lettering on the white destination blind is worthy of note.

G R Mills

HL 5335 (top right)
Looking somewhat tired after 24 years service, the Leyland TD2 is seen at rest in March 1956 in St Johns Street bus station, Colchester, with Abbeygate Street in the background. Withdrawn 6 months later, the bus was sold to Honeywood of Stanstead, and gave a another years service before final retirement at 25.

G R Mills

BEL 391 (second from top right)
The more spritely 16-year old Leyland TD4/Brush rests on Stand 20 in Colchester's St Johns Street bus station in July 1956 with a Norfolk's of Nayland Bedford OB (ACF 669) on the Saturday service to Higham alongside. The TD4 was sold to Honeywood a year later and survived into the ownership of Goldsmiths of Sicklesmere.

G R Mills

NV 5141 (third from top right)
This smart Leyland TD4/ECW also rests on Stand 20 in Colchester's St Johns Street bus station in May 1956. A Norfolk's OB (CUJ 654) and Best's Leyland TD5 (ADR 795) await their departures alongside. The advert on the side of the bus reads "To read the label stand this bus up on end ... (Guinness for Strength)". The same slogan is on HL 5335 above.

G R Mills

FEV 182 (bottom right)
One of a pair of Leyland TD5/ECW operated for six years into Colchester is seen at the Halstead terminus in Factory lane West ion October 1961. Note that the Guinness advertising has been tamed to "Pass right down inside" considerably less strenuous than the challenge on HL and NV!

G R Mills

EUH 973 (bottom left)
This was one of a pair of Leyland PD2s acquired to replace the TD5s, which were the last double-deckers to join the Blackwell fleet as both passed to Hedingham Omnibuses in October 1965. This scene in December 1963 shows the PD2 leading FEV 182 out of Halstead Road into London Road, Lexden, the TD5 having duplicated the Halstead - Colchester service from Earls Colne.

G R Mills

H G Boon, Church Road, Boreham, Essex

Coaching commenced in May 1949 with pre-war Bedfords followed by post-war Bedford OB/Duple Vistas. The first new coach was an odd Guy Otter with Withnell bodywork in June 1958. However, Bedfords continued to dominate, both new and used, until February 1972 when a new Seddon Pennine 6/Plaxton Elite was delivered. The Seddon's first regular driver, Alan Goodwin, bought the coach 8 years later to add to his own fleet based near Braintree. Goodwin sold his business to Wicks of Braintree in May 2006.

School contracts and bingo runs prompted the introduction of double-deckers. Experience with Leyland engines in Bedford and Atlanteans led to the purchase of used Bristol LHL coaches and later new LHS and LH models. Launching heavily into the executive coach market, the purchase of two used Setra S215 was followed by a further second-hand model and seven brand-new examples. Six of the latter passed to Windmill Coaches of Copford in April 1999 when Mark Boon dropped out of coaches in favour of an all double-deck fleet working only on school contract journeys. At the same time the smart premises were sold for housing development and the fleet moved to a rented yard on Boreham Industrial Estate, as Boons Buses.

Following a fleet check by Ministry of Transport vehicle examiners at schools in the Chelmsford area in 2003 (including Chelmer Valley High, St John Payne and Sandon) the operators licence was revoked and consequently Essex County Council cancelled all the school contracts. Furthermore the fleet was impounded at Boreham for several weeks before repossessed by Ensignbus, whilst the two newest ex-Colchester Atlantean/ECW were acquired by Talisman of Great Bromley - one for conversion to open-top, the other as a heritage bus in original Colchester Borough Transport livery.

Livery: cream and maroon

Double-Deckers operated 1973 - 2003

Reg	Chassis	Body	Seats	New	In	Ex	Out
RUF 205	Leyland PD2/12	East Lancs	H33/26R	1955	8/73	Kenzie, Shepreth	12/73
NCK 365	Leyland PDR1/1	MCW	H44/34F	1959	12/73	Blueline, Upminster	12/80
579 RKJ	Leyland PDR1/1	Metro-Cammell	H44/33F	1961	9/75	Maidstone & District (5579)	9/79
EKP 234C	Leyland PDR1/1	Massey	H43/34F	1965	4/77	Maidstone (34)	3/88
CYS 568B	Leyland PDR1/1	Alexander	H43/34F	1964	8/77	Greater Glasgow PTE (LA222)	10/81
KBB 246D	Leyland PDR1/1	Alexander	H43/34F	1966	9/77	Tyne & Wear PTE (1446)	4/80
JSC 883E	Leyland PDR1/1	Alexander	H43/31F	1967	7/80	Lothian (883)	2/99
SPW 92N	Leyland AN68/2R	Roe	H45/33F	1974	9/80	Pegg, Caston	6/99
BCS 962C	Daimler CRG6LX	Alexander	H44/31F	1965	9/80	Western SMT (1979)	12/80
TGX 704M	Daimler CRL6	Park Royal	H44/32D	1973	11/80	London Transport (DMS704)	10/91
KUC 245P	Daimler CRL6	MCW	H44/32D	1975	7/81	London Transport (DM1245)	11/81
MVK 538R	Leyland AN68A/2R	Alexander	H48/34F	1976	11/90	Colchester (51)	1/02
NNO 66P	Leyland AN68A/1R	ECW	H43/31F	1976	6/91	Colchester (66)	9/02
NNO 63P	Leyland AN68A/1R	ECW	H43/31F	1976	10/91	Colchester (63)	7/03
YNO 78S	Leyland AN68A/1R	ECW	H43/31F	1978	9/98	Colchester (78)	7/03
XPG 182T	Leyland AN68A/1R	Park Royal	H43/30F	1978	2/99	Arriva West Surrey (AN182)	7/03
VPA 149S	Leyland AN68A/1R	Park Royal	H43/30F	1978	5/99	Nu Venture, Aylesford	7/03
RVW 90W	Leyland AN68A/1R	ECW	H43/31F	1980	3/00	Arriva Colchester (5302)	7/03
B146 WUL	MCW DR101/17	MCW	H43/28D	1985	11/01	Metroline (M146)	7/03
KYO 628X	MCW DR101/14	MCW	H43/28D	1981	1/02	Arriva London North (M628)	7/03

Notes:
RUF 205 was new to Southdown (805)
NCK 365 was new to Ribble (1624)
MVK 538R was new to Tyne & Wear PTE (538)
VPA 149S and XPG 182T were new to London Country (AN149/82)

KYO 628X and B146 WUL were new to London Transport (M628, M1146)

RUF 205, EKP 234C, JSC 883E and RVW 90W survived into preservation

(Ref: *Buses* 313 April 1981)

Left to right: KBB 246D, EKP 234C, CYS 568B, NCK 365
Boons's Atlanteans parade in January 1980 at the Riverside Leisure Centre in Victoria Road, Chelmsford. Bodywork is by Alexander, Massey, Alexander and MCW; all are in livery with fleetname lettering.
G R Mills

RUF 205 (top left)

After 24 years as a coach operator, Boon's bought this superb Leyland PD2 from the equally well-kept fleet of Kenzies when the latter ceased double-decker operation in 1973. The classic bus is seen still in Kenzies blue livery on return to the deport at Boreham after working a school contract during October 1973.

G R Mills

579 RKJ (second from top left)

The second of six Leyland Atlantean PDR1/1 types that graced the Boon fleet awaits Buxton chicken factory workers in November 1975. This bus ended its days as engineless control box on a stock car track at Felsted until the Braintree to Stansted dual carriageway was built which cut through the site.

G R Mills

JSC 883E (third from top left)

Hector Boon's son Mark was over at Hadleigh in Suffolk the day after 8 of the 12 Atlantean/Alexander buses from Edinburgh arrived at Partridge's depot. His choice was justified as the chosen bus outlived all the other PDR/1/1s, giving nearly19 years service. The smart bus is seen in October 1988 loading Buxton chicken factory workers.

G R Mills

NNO 66P (third from top left)

Another bus that was to achieve a long life, after nearly 11 years at Boons, it went to Emblings of Guyhirn joining 18 Bristol VRTs with the same style of ECW body. Always well presented, the bus was a credit to the owner as this January 1992 view shows.

G R Mills

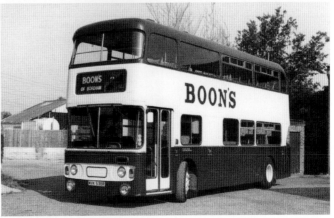

TGX 704M (top right)

Rather than block the centre door, Hector Boon had the front entrance reduced to gain an extra pair of seats, creating a unique DMS as seen at the depot in August 1983.

G R Mills

MVK 538R (bottom right)

Removal of the centre door, obvious in this August 1991 view, was completed in Newcastle for Colchester Borough Transport when three of the batch were acquired in 1983. The largest double-decker in the Boon's fleet ended its days as a storeshed and source of spares at Dons, Dunmow.

G R Mills

A F Braybrooke & Son, King Road, Mendlesham, Suffolk

An exceptional psv operation with many rare features stretching over two counties Braybrooke's was. founded in 1946 by the acquisition of the 5-vehicle fleet of W T Jarvis of Swaffham. The fleet was upgraded by the purchase of three AEC Q coaches from Sutton's of Clacton and by a trio of new Crossley coaches. However a month before the second Crossley was delivered the premises and eight vehicles of Tye Brothers of Mendlesham were acquired, in October 1949. The adjoining house was occupied by A W Braybrooke, who administered both bases, which were some 50 miles apart. Another odd purchase was a pair of Strachans bodied Morris-Commercial coaches which were operated for twelve years. Later the fleet became well-known for the acquisition of seven AEC Regal III/Harrington coaches from Maidstone & District which were employed on American school contracts to various USAF bases in East Anglia.

The Swaffham operations and the Regent garage premises on the main Fakenham road, passed to Colin S Pegg of Caston in 1964 although no vehicles changed hands. The original garage was demolished to make way for a petrol filling station and a new workshop was erected well back from the A1065 road. By the time Pegg's operations ceased in February 1995, the Swaffham premises had passed to a tyre and exhaust firm.

The Mendlesham operations were considerably more successful with a regular intake of new Bedford coaches from 1956 to 1977. On the contract output, double-deckers could be employed on English school journeys but were taboo on any American ones. A W Braybrooke realised the double-decker had potential and based one each at Swaffham and Mendlesham. When the former base was sold, the double-decker went south to Suffolk and occasionally appeared on the stage service into Stowmarket.

A "Woofer" Braybrooke was a charismatic man of diverse interests. His personal transport between the two depots was an E-type Jaguar, a keen aviator he held a pilots licence and also owned Wetheringsett Manor Hotel (later a religious centre). The business was sold to Touranglia Ltd (John and Roger Stedman) of Sudbury, Suffolk in March 1978 but was renamed Galloway European Coachlines Ltd seven months later, adopting the green livery of the parent company, County Travel (Leicester) Ltd.

Galloway moved into purpose built premises at Denters Hill on the Stowmarket side of the village on 2 January 1990. Whilst getting the workshop facilities fully operational the old Braybrooke garage and a unit in Station Road were also utilised. When these were no longer required, the original workshop, offices and covered parking area were demolished to make way for a housing development. A tribute to the long-term occupant of the site still exists as the rear access road is named Braybrooke Close.

Livery: red and cream

Double-Deckers operated 1960 - 1964

Reg	Chassis	Body	Seats	New	In	Ex	Out
JEH 474	Guy Arab II	NCME	L26/26R	1943	9/60	Potteries (L240)	9/64
EX 5263	Guy Arab II	Strachan	H30/26R	1945	9/61	Great Yarmouth (16)	9/62

Note - JEH 474 originally had a Strachan L27/28R body, the NCME body was fitted in 1952

JEH 474
The smartly repainted Northern Counties bodied Guy Arab II is seen at the King Road depot, alongside the proprietors home in May 1964. The bus had previously worked at the Swaffham depot prior to transfer to Mendlesham to join a Guy Arab with an original Strachan utility body similar to that previously fitted to JEH 474.
                    G R Mills

Corona Coaches Ltd, Old Market Place, Sudbury, Suffolk

Alan A Chinery of Acton founded the Corona Coaches business in 1928 with a new 16 seat Chevrolet. In May 1929 he bravely started a Stowmarket to London service utilising a new 32 seat Gilford delivered the previous month. After the introduction of the Road Traffic Act, licences were held for daily services to Stowmarket; a Thursday and Saturday route from Acton to Sudbury and a Tuesday (market day) service from Sudbury to Ipswich. Significantly, the fleet intake was consistently new; from 1931-1939 fourteen were delivered, and, after World War II from 1945 - 1953 a further dozen entered the fleet.

On 1 February 1956 the management changed together with policies. Only three months later, the 4-vehicle business of Harry Rippingale, Gestingthorpe, Essex was acquired with stage services linking the villages in his area with Sudbury, Halstead and Braintree. Further expansion followed on 18 August 1956 when the bus business of A J Long of Glemsford was amalgamated with Corona adding 10 vehicles, including 3 double-deckers, to the fleet. The latter trio, all attired in dark blue and white livery, were employed on weekdays on the daily service between Clare and Sudbury. The Long merger also took Corona stock into Bury St Edmunds on a daily basis.

The company ceased trading on 9 August 1959. Theobalds, Long Melford took over the former Long's services; A E Letch of Sible Hedingham acquired the ex Rippingale routes; N S Rule, Boxford, the original Chinery routes whilst the London service passed to Mulley's Motorways of Ixworth. Corona was perpetuated as a fleetname on Mulley's cream and orange vehicles and both the Acton garage and the Sudbury office were used. The London service later passed to Eastern Counties (from 4 November 1962) and the Sudbury office passed to Winch & Blatch as a retail wine store. Whilst the Acton garage survived beyond 1981, when the Mulley's Motorways business was sold to the Munson family (owners of Beeston's of Hadleigh), the site was eventually sold for housing.

Livery: chocolate brown and tangerine orange

Double-Deckers operated 1958 - 1959 (all ex Long, Glemsford in August 1958)

	Reg	Chassis	Body	Seats	New	In	Previously	Out
32	GHU 489	Bristol K5G	Brush	L26/26R	1941	8/58	Southern Vectis (785)	9/59
33	DSG 168	AEC Regent	Brush	L27/28R	1942	8/58	SMT (BB2)	9/59
34	CFW 212	Guy Arab II	Roe	L27/28R	1945	8/58	Lincolnshire (1716)	9/59

A J Long, Hunts Hill, Glemsford, Suffolk
Livery: dark blue and white

Double-Deckers operated 1951 - 1958 (withdrawn prior to acquisition by Corona)

Reg	Chassis	Body	Seats	New	In	Ex	Out
ARU 164	Leyland TD4	Brush	L27/26R	1935	6/51	Hants & Dorset (969)	7/58
BEL 395	Leyland TD4c	Brush	L27/26R	1935	3/53	Hants & Dorset (999)	8/55

Note - GHU 489 was new to Bristol (3352) and originally had a Bristol H30/26R body, the Brush body was fitted in 1943

CFW 212
All three of the double-deckers taken into stock by Corona, ex-Longs, were repainted into the distinctive brown and orange as shown on the utility Guy passing "The Bull" in Long Melford in March 1959 on a well loaded journey from Glemsford. Only six months later all the double-deckers were withdrawn and none ever saw psv service again.

R A Jenkinson/G R Mills collection

Culling & Son (Norwich) Ltd, Mill Garage, Claxton, Norfolk

The name of Culling was synonymous with Norwich for over 50 years. In pre-war years the fleetname "Claxton & District" was used, but the post war intake of three new Dennis Lancets and 4 new TSM half cabs prompted the adoption of the "Culling's Radio Coaches" fleetname which was signwritten along the side of the roof panels. A mill logo normally appeared in a circle on the side panels as a windmill existed on the Claxton site until the outbreak of World war II when the landmark was demolished. Nothing now remains of the Claxton premises as the site was redeveloped for housing.

In the early post war years, the patronage on the daily service into Norfolk's capital city was overloading the Bedford OWB buses, which justified the acquisition of two double-deckers. From 1953 to 1958, two AEC and five Bedford coaches purchased new had "800" in their registration marks as Arthur Culling's first new car, a 1949 Vauxhall Velox, was HPW 800 (a registration which preceded a batch of Eastern Counties Beadle-Bedfords, HPW 801-816 and the unique Dennis/ECW batch HPW 817-32). An additional office functioned at Ber Street in the city where the stage service from Hardley terminated on a daily basis. In the same period, coach operation was buoyant so Culling's acquired the largest Norwich based business, Red Car Service, in October 1959. Although the red and grey livery was maintained on the acquired stock, evidence of the takeover was obvious as new AEC and Bedford coaches entered service with "800" marks.

In 1980 the combined operation was sold to the Margo family with the proviso that the Culling name was discontinued and everything licensed to the Red Car Service (Norwich) Ltd. However this was short-lived as the receivers were called in during August 1981. Anglian of Loddon (later at Ellough) acquired the stage service while JDW Transport of Ipswich made a brave attempt to cope with the coaching duties until they too ceased to trade in December 1981. In January 1983, a new enterprise took over the Ber Street office, T M Smith, using the trading name Y C Travel and fleetname Norfolk Bluebird.

Livery: grey, yellow and white

Double-Deckers operated 1960 - 1964

Reg	Chassis	Body		Seats	New	In	Ex	Out
ED 6562	Leyland TD1	Brush		H30/26R	1931	11/47	Warrington (29)	1/53
HL 9063	Leyland TD5c	Roe		L24/24R	1939	6/49	West Riding (534)	4/53
FNW 708	Leyland TD5c	Roe		H31/25R	1937	1/52	Leeds (308)	8/60
CRU 704	Leyland TD4	Brush		L27/26R	1937	9/52	Hants & Dorset (1008)	1/56
CRN 59	Daimler CVD6	Strachan		L27/28R	1949	4/53	Viking, Preston	7/57
DLU 406	Leyland TD4c	Leyland		H30/26R	1937	7/55	London Transport (STD96)	8/60
DCR 685	Guy Arab I	Brush		L27/26R	1943	8/57	Alexander Greyhound, Sheffield	12/62
JUO563	AEC Regent III	Weymann		H30/26R	1948	7/60	Devon General (DR563)	7/69
OTW 922	AEC Regent III	Weymann		H30/26R	1949	12/62	Shell, Thames Haven	12/68
HWW 874	Bristol K6B	ECW		L27/28R	1950	1/65	West Yorkshire (DB47)	7/72
WNO 482	Bristol KSW5G	ECW		O33/28R	1953	3/73	Eastern Counties (LKO239)	12/81
VVF 215	Bristol LD5G	ECW		H33/27R	1958	7/75	Eastern Counties (LKD215)	8/79
DAU 434C	Leyland PDR1/1	Metro-Cammell	H44/33F		1965	4/77	Nottingham (434)	9/79

Notes:
DCR 865 was new to Hants & Dorset (CD954 later 1101)
VVF 215 was part of the Red Car fleet under Culling ownership

WNO 482 was new to Eastern National (4204, later 1424, later 2381) and was licensed to the Red Car fleet from 4/81

WNO 482

Originally a standard Eastern National KSW with ECW L27/28R body, WNO 482 was converted to open-top in 1966 and worked at Claxton before transfer to Eastern Counties in 1968 to work between Cromer and Sheringham. Seen here as a participant in the annual Ipswich to Felixstowe road run in May 1973 on the seafront near the Spa Pavilion, the bus was later repainted white and red under Margo ownership and lettered Red Car. When the fleet was auctioned off in December 1981 the bus was sold to Abel's Removals of Watton, Norfolk, repainted blue and fitted with a demountable part roof to act as control tower at events at the Norfolk Showground.

G R Mills

DCR 865 (top left)
One of nine Ministry of Supply specification Guy Arabs delivered to Hants & Dorset in 1942/3, 865 was the only Brush bodied example in the set. The results of a rebuild by Portsmouth Aviation in December 1949 can be clearly seen in this September 1961 view in Ber Street, Norwich - rubber glazed windows, sliding side vents (ex half drops), rebuilt destination layout and rounded roof dome. The cobbled street and old style "Keep Left" sign are worthy of note.

G R Mills

OTW 922 (second from top left)
An unusual source provided this AEC Regent III/Weymann, a former non-psv staff transport bus at Shell Petroleum's Thames Haven refinery. The bus was virtually identical to JUO 563, an ex-Devon General example purchased two years earlier. The body design is very similar to the London lowbridge RLH class even though the Culling's examples were both full-height as seen in this March 1968 view of a well-loaded OTW 922 departing Ber Street.

G R Mills

HWY 874 (third from top left)
Many ex-West Yorkshire Bristol Ks were acquired by East Anglian operators, mostly via W North of Leeds (later at Sherburn-in-Elmet). The type was prolific in the territory with green Eastern National and red Eastern Counties examples thus a grey, yellow and white version was refreshingly different as can be visualised by this September 1966 view in Ber Street. The ownership link with Red Car service is clearly shown on the side advert panel. The bus was subsequently repainted maroon by Riverway, Harlow.

G R Mills

VVF 215
The last rear-entrance double-decker purchased was painted in Red Car Service red, grey and white but the Culling ownership is demonstrated by the large lettering on the side advert panel. The previous ownership is obvious by the Eastern Counties style "Norwich Bus Station" on the destination blind as seen in Ber Street in April 1979.

G R Mills

DAU 434C
The first rear-engined/front-entrance double-decker purchased was also the last ever to join the Culling fleet as the service to Hardley and district was subsequently operated by AEC saloons. The last of the line is seen arriving at the Ber Street terminus outside Bonds (later John Lewis) department store in September 1978. The old English fleetname lettering survived to the end of double-deck operation.

G R Mills

G E Dack (t/a Rosemary Coaches), Northgate Way, Terrington St Clement, Norfolk

George Dack started in the PSV world in a modest way early in 1958 with an ex-Wallace Arnold Leyland Tiger PS1. In the ensuing 10 years, a further four Leyland models were acquired from the same source. A particular type that found great favour were Leyland Tiger Cubs with Plaxton C41F bodies, new to Smiths of Wigan with DJP registrations as eight were acquired, none direct although 4 came via Hills of Tredegar.

The Leyland marque predominated in the fleet strength with over 90 being owned during the 35 years of operation. The only brand new coaches ever purchased were three Tigers in the 1980s. Ironically, in 1971 when the first double-decker was needed to work the ex Doughty service from Kings Lynn to Magdalen, a Gardner 6LW engined Guy was acquired. When rear engined double-deckers became available in quantity on the second-hand market, Gardner powered units featured prominently in Dack's choices.

The "Rosemary" fleetname was derived from the Christian name of George's daughter; too young to be involved in the business at the outset, but by the time of George's untimely death in 1988 she was running the operation together with her brother Colin through to the sale to Eastern Counties in June 1993.

In the early days, the coaches were parked in the old Terrington St Clement station yard, (a former Midland & Great Northern Joint Railway property on the Lynn - Spalding line) moving later to the Emorsgate shed/yard also in the village. Doughty's premises at St Michaels Road in Kings Lynn were used as well from 1979. The latter premises were retained by Eastern Counties but later redeveloped.

At the peak of Dack's operations, the double-deckers covered the English school contracts and stage journeys whilst the coaches were to be seen some distance away from the Kings Lynn area with many American school children conveyed on contracts for USAF personnel at the Alconbury (Cambs), Lakenheath (Suffolk) and Sculthorpe (Norfolk) bases. This involved vehicles being outstationed well south of the home base operating centre.

Double-Deckers operated 1971 - 1993

Reg	Chassis	Body	Seats	New	In	Ex	Out
GFN 918	Guy Arab IV	Park Royal	H30/26RD	1953	7/71	East Kent	11/72
212 BPU	Bristol LD5G	ECW	H33/25R	1955	11/72	Eastern National (2420)	1/75
903 LRR	Leyland PD2/1	NCME	FL37/33F	1961	3/75	Barton (903)	3/76
JHW 62E	Bristol FLF6B	ECW	H38/32F	1967	9/80	Bristol (7294)	5/87
JHW 61E	Bristol FLF6B	ECW	H38/32F	1967	3/81	Bristol (7293)	5/87
5014 VT	Daimler CRG6LX	Alexander	H41/31F	1964	8/81	PMT (1014)	8/85
5019 VT	Daimler CRG6LX	Alexander	H41/31F	1964	8/81	PMT (1019)	8/86
DNF 705C	Daimler CRG6LX	Metro-Cammell	H43/32F	1965	9/82	Greater Manchester (4705)	2/88
GHA 430D	Daimler CRG6LX	Alexander	H44/33F	1966	9/82	Heyfordian, Upper Heyford	2/86
BHL 620K	Daimler CRG6LX	NCME	H43/33F	1972	9/84	West Riding (720)	6/89
BHL 628K	Daimler CRG6LX	NCME	H43/33F	1972	9/84	West Riding (728)	6/90
BWB 140H	Leyland PDR2/1	Park Royal	H47/32D	1964	11/84	Smith, Sacriston	2/88
GYJ 399G	Daimler CRG6LX	Alexander	H43/34F	1969	2/86	McLennan, Spittalfield	12/87
GYJ 403G	Daimler CRG6LX	Alexander	H44/34F	1969	2/86	McLennan, Spittalfield	5/90
CKC 302L	Daimler CRG6LXB	MCW	H43/32F	1973	5/87	Crosville (HDG934)	6/93
CKC 312L	Daimler CRG6LXB	MCW	H43/32F	1973	10/87	Crosville (HDG938)	6/93
PXA 637J	Daimler CRG6LXB	ECW	H43/34F	1971	11/87	Highland Scottish (D320)	4/91
UAG 133J	Daimler CRG6LXB	NCME	H44/31F	1971	11/87	Highland Scottish (D328)	4/91
WWH 26L	Daimler CRG6LXB	Park Royal	H43/32F	1973	5/88	GM Buses (7168)	6/93
GAG 48N	Bristol VRT/SL2/6LX	ECW	H39/31F	1974	6/89	East Yorkshire (941)	6/93
GNS 672N	Leyland AN68/1R	Alexander	H45/31F	1975	3/90	Kentish Bus (646)	5/90
OJD 195R	Leyland FE30AGR	MCW	H45/32F	1977	5/90	Derby (249)	6/93
YHN 654M	Bristol VRT/SL2/6LX	ECW	H43/31F	1974	5/90	Ribble (2046)	6/93
THX 531S	Leyland Fleetline	Park Royal	H44/27D	1977	3/91	London Buses (DMS2531)	6/93
THX 573S	Leyland Fleetline	Park Royal	H44/27D	1977	3/91	London Buses (DMS2523)	6/93

Notes:

903 LRR was a Barton BTD2 rebuild from ex Yorkshire Woollen HD 7832

GHA 430D was new to Midland Red (6030)

BWB 140H was new to Sheffield (740)

GYJ 399G and GYJ 403G were new to Dundee (299, 303)

CKC 302L and CKC 312L were new to Merseyside PTE (3002/12)

PXA 637J was new to Alexander (Fife) (RF37)

UAG 133J was new to Western SMT (R2290)

GNS 372N was new to Strathclyde PTE (LA880)

GFN 918 (top left)

This classic Park Royal bodied Guy Arab was still in full East Kent livery when about to leave the Millfleet bus park in Kings Lynn in October 1971. Despite the fact that the bus is bound for Madgalen on the ex-Doughty service, the destination blind reads "Folkestone Wood Avenue", however local ownership is confirmed by the Rosemary Coaches fleetname on the side panels.

G R Mills

212 BPU (second left)

The second double-decker in the Dack fleet was fully repainted into red and cream in an attractive style as this view in Kings Lynn's Millfleet bus park shows. The ecclesiastical styled building to the right is in fact the town's library whilst a very basic bus shelter can be seen at the rear. The Lodekka carries fleet number B3 although it was the fifth Bristol to join the strength, being preceded by four LS models.

G R Mills

JHW 62E (top right)

After a four-year period without any double-deckers in the fleet, a pair of ex Bristol Omnibus FLF6Bs were acquired from W North, Sherburn-in-Elmet. This one was freshly repainted, as can be seen by the smart wheels and wings, in this September 1980 view at Kings Lynn's out of town market area. At the rear, Dack's only Daimler Roadliner/Plaxton, ex-Black & White of Cheltenham, can be seen displaying some trophies. Six years later, the pair were traded back to North's for two ex-Merseyside Fleetlines (see below).

G R Mills

CKC 312L (bottom right)

In June 1993, Eastern Counties acquired the Dack fleet, which included the pair of Merseyside Fleetlines among eight double-deckers. Little had changed when caught in the Vancouver Centre bus station in Kings Lynn during February 1994 apart from fleet number DD508 barely discernible below the centre of the front windscreen. Neither vehicle ever received Eastern Counties livery. At the rear is a Bird's of Hunstanton Ford/Plaxton on a market day service, the operation of which passed to Sanders of Holt in August 1998 together with the fleet. An Eastern Counties Dennis Javelin/Plaxton bus is visible in the background.

G R Mills

R Doughty & Sons (Coaches) Ltd, Jermyn Road, Kings Lynn, Norfolk

Doughty's daily service into Kings Lynn (Millfleet) was of particular interest as double-deckers, from the early fifties to early seventies, consistently provided the weekday journeys. There were several other independent operators running into Kings Lynn but most of their services only ran on Tuesdays (market day) and Saturdays: Bunn of Walsingham; Carter, Litcham; Carter, Marham; Carter, Northwold; Eagle, Castle Acre and Parnell of West Rudham never operated double-deckers while Braybrooke, Swaffham; Matthews Blue, Shouldham and Towler of Emneth rarely used anything but coaches on their services.

Another feature of Doughty's double-deck fleet was the use of ex London RTL class buses purchased via Bird's of Stratford-upon-Avon - the lion's share of this class had been exported to Ceylon (Sri Lanka) and the RT class (AEC Regent III) was three times larger in numbers. Doughty's even sampled one from the vast quantity of this type.

The last new coaches purchased were a pair of Bedford SB5/Duple Bella Vega C41F, both of which passed to Partridge of Hadleigh when the business closed in January 1979, by which time the largest coaches operated were 45-seaters. The depot in St Michaels Road was leased to George Dack (t/a Rosemary Coaches) from 1979 but the stage services had already been acquired by Dack's in 1971.

When the Dack business failed in June 1993, Eastern Counties acquired the assets including the vehicles and used the ex-Doughty premises until September 2002 when all the operations were transferred to their depot in Vancouver Avenue and the Vancouver Centre bus station.

Livery: dark green and white

Double-Deckers operated 1953 - 1979

Reg	Chassis	Body	Seats	New	In	Ex	Out
FOF 318	Leyland TD6c	Leyland	H28/24R	1939	2/53	Birmingham (1318)	3/58
FOF 270	Leyland TD6c	Leyland	H28/24R	1939	7/54	Birmingham (1270)	7/55
FOF 294	Leyland TD6c	Leyland	H28/24R	1939	1/55	Birmingham (1294)	4/58
GKL 764	Leyland TD7	Weymann	H28/26R	1940	7/56	Maidstone & District (DH6)	4/58
JXN 318	Leyland 7RT	Park Royal	H30/26R	1948	3/58	London Transport (RTL6)	4/68
JXN 319	Leyland 7RT	Park Royal	H30/26R	1948	3/58	London Transport (RTL7)	9/69
JXN 321	Leyland 7RT	Park Royal	H30/26R	1948	3/58	London Transport (RTL9)	9/69
HLX 328	AEC Regent III	Park Royal	H30/26R	1948	7/63	London Transport (RT611)	9/69
KGK 911	Leyland 7RT	Park Royal	H30/26R	1949	9/68	London Transport (RTL247)	6/72
KGK 908	Leyland 7RT	Weymann	H30/26R	1949	3/69	London Transport (RTL244)	6/72
VTX 435	AEC Regent V	Weymann	H39/31F	1957	3/72	Western Welsh (435)	3/77
YJG 820	AEC Regent V	Park Royal	H40/32F	1962	3/77	East Kent	6/79

JXN 321 (right)

One of the trio of ex-London RTL class which replaced the regular ex-Birmingham Leyland TD6s on the main service to Magdalen via St Germans is seen loading in Kings Lynn's Millfleet bus park in August 1961. Note the classic 1935 Rover parked on the opposite side of the road outside the Stonegate Hotel.

G R Mills

VTX 435 (left)

The first front-entranced double-decker in the fleet, smartly repainted into Doughty's green and white, rests at the St Michaels Road yard in September 1973. The large building in the background is Lawes fertilisers warehouse which was later evacuated and left derelict for a long time before finally being demolished.

G R Mills

16

R E Howard (t/a Halstead Travel), 12 Tweed Close, Halstead, Essex

For a small market town, Halstead has had an array of private operators during the post-war years including A G Frost, licensee of the White Horse (1959-1976); A Monty (t/a Halstead Coaches) (1974-1977) and Ron Howard, who traded as Halstead Travel from 1993 to 2003. Ron was a one-time Hedingham Omnibuses driver before venturing into business as a taxi and coach owner. Commencing operations with Bedford YRTs, he progressed through YMT models to a YNT, normally buying and selling through other local operators such as Partridges of Hadleigh. When double-deckers were required for school contracts all were obtained from and returned, when the work was lost, to Phil Munson at Beeston's also in Hadleigh. The vehicles were variously parked in the former Blackwell's yard in Coggeshall Road, Earls Colne; Sudbury Road, Little Maplestead, West Mead Industrial Estate, Gosfield; as well as Butler Road, Halstead.

In July 1998 Ron commenced weekday service 88H from Great Yeldham to Colchester via Halstead and Earls Colne in direct competition with his former employer. Initially Bedford/Plaxton coaches were the regular performers but in the twilight years the allocation changed to a Mercedes midi-bus. Following a purge by Ministry of Transport vehicle inspectors in Colchester Bus Station, the fleet attracted some prohibition orders, which eventually led to the operators' licence being revoked in June 2003, although the service had ended abruptly in November 2002. The double-deckers had been employed on school contracts, which included a service from Honywood School, Coggeshall to Colne Engaine Green.

Livery: blue and white

Double-Deckers operated 1997- 1998

Reg	Chassis	Body	Seats	New	In	Ex	Out
BUH 233V	Bristol VRT/SL3/6LXB	ECW	H40/27F	1980	8/97	Southend (381)	8/98
LHG 440T	Bristol VRT/SL3/501	ECW	H43/31F	1979	8/97	Southend (401)	1/98
DWY 146T	Bristol VRT/SL3/6LXB	ECW	H43/31F	1979	8/97	Southend (304)	2/98
PKM 113R	Bristol VRT/SL3/6LXB	ECW	H43/31F	1977	1/98	Maidstone & District (5113)	12/98

Notes:
BUH 233V was new to National Welsh (LR8005)   DWY 146T was new to West Riding (412)
LHG 440T was new to Ribble (1440)

DWY 146T (left)
Seen at Beeston's yard in Long Bessels, Hadleigh (cleared in 2005), the source of its sale and return in 1998. The upper deck and staircase panel has suffered after the removal of the "L" shaped advert, revealing West Riding's red paintwork. Southend Transport were obviously emphatic about "no smoking" as every window has a reminder label!

G R Mills

LHG 440T (right)
Originally one of 23 (LHG 437-59T) new to Ribble between December 1978 and June 1979, the batch was unusual in being of highbridge layout and having Leyland 501 engines. Later one of four which passed to Southend Transport, the short-lived school bus is seen at the Swimming Pool Car Park in Hadleigh, Suffolk, in January 1998, still in Southend livery.

G R Mills

F Goldsmith (Sicklesmere) Ltd, The Garage, Sicklesmere, Suffolk

For over 30 years, the founder, Fred Goldsmith, owned the business until the premises, vehicles and operations were sold to the Brewster family in August 1949. The sale included three Bedford OWB buses which had been allocated new during WW2 due to the proximity of RAF stations in the area. The new owners continued a policy of purchasing new coaches, the first, a Vulcan 6PF with Dutfield bodywork, was still on site 55 years later. Another quirk was the consistent issue of triple numbers in the registration marks over the subsequent 32 years, such that all combinations from 111 to 999, four twice over but never a 555, appeared on a dozen coaches supplied new, all with Plaxton bodies and all, bar one, on Bedford chassis.

Expansion followed with acquisition of Turner, Rattlesden in April 1955, with two Bedford OB/Duples being added to the fleet. The largest boost to the operations was the purchase of the fleet of F J Honeywood, Stanstead, which included stage services from Glemsford in March 1958. This took the Goldsmith fleet from 9 to 16 vehicles and included two double-deckers. These were required to operate the weekday journeys on the daily service from Glemsford to Bury St Edmunds, which on Wednesdays (market day) even required reliefs on part of the route. However within 10 years the loadings had declined to the extent that a 41-seat coach coped adequately. After a 5-year gap during which no double-deckers were operated, school contract demands dictated the need for larger capacity but the decline in patronage on the stage services continued. Unfortunately the proprietor crossed swords with the Ministry of Transport and the operator's licence was revoked in December 1992. Ironically both the second Honeywood and the last Goldsmith double-deckers have been saved with WH 1553 going initially to Leyland Motors Ltd and later to the Lincolnshire Vintage Vehicle Society at North Hykeham in 1969. ROC 300R, some 48 years newer, was acquired by the Birmingham and Midland Museum of Transport at Wythall.

Honeywood's premises were sold for housing development and no evidence now exists of their operations in the village of Stanstead. Goldsmith's forecourt at Sicklesmere was eventually cleared, after the Foden had stood idle by the unused petrol pumps for over 15 years and twice been hit by passing cars in the winter months, for occupation by Carson Cars, a secondhand vehicle dealer. However the entire remaining stock was disused on the premises, some having been withdrawn 20 years before operations ceased.

Livery: duo blue and cream

Double-Deckers operated 1954 - 1985

Reg	Chassis	Body	Seats	New	In	Ex	Out
CXX 379	AEC Regent	LPTB	H30/26R	1936	5/54	London Transport (STL1690)	7/56
BEL 391	Leyland TD4	Brush	L27/26R	1935	3/58	Honeywood, Stanstead	3/59
CWM 571	Leyland TD5c	ECW	L27/26R	1937	3/58	Honeywood, Stanstead	9/60
ASD 834	Daimler CWA6	Duple	L27/26R	1945	12/58	Wesley, Stoke Goldington	11/61
GUF 37	Guy Arab II	East Lancs	H28/26R	1943	9/59	Southdown (407)	11/61
XG 8203	Leyland PD1	Roe	H31/25R	1946	9/59	Irvine, Salsburgh	1/69
GNY 769	AEC Regent III	Weymann	H30/26R	1947	9/59	Rhondda (223)	1/64
HTG 701	AEC Regent III	Weymann	H30/26R	1948	9/59	Rhondda (233)	12/61
DEV 479	Bristol GO5G	ECW	L27/28R	1936	4/62	Eastern National (1239)	3/64
GPW 349	Leyland PD1A	ECW	L27/26R	1947	1/64	Eastern Counties (AP349)	1/67
GPW 347	Leyland PD1A	ECW	L27/26R	1947	3/64	Eastern Counties (AP347)	3/68
309 MFC	AEC Bridgemaster	Park Royal	H43/29F	1961	4/74	Oxford (309)	11/78
AJA 118B	AEC Renown	Park Royal	H42/30F	1964	6/78	Blatchly, Stevenage	11/79
SOE 956H	Daimler CRG6LX	Park Royal	H47/33D	1969	11/79	Partridge, Hadleigh	12/85
ROC 300R	Foden 6LXB	NCME	H43/33F	1977	6/83	West Midlands PTE (6300)	6/85

F J Honeywood, The Garage, Stanstead, Suffolk
Livery: brown and cream

Double-Deckers operated 1940 - 1957 (sold prior to acquisition by Goldsmith's)

Reg	Chassis	Body	Seats	New	In	Ex	Out
HD 3699	Leyland TD1	Leyland	L26/26R	1928	10/45	Sprackling, Blandford	8/49
WH 1553	Leyland TD1	Leyland	L27/24R	1929	11/47	Hicks, Braintree (53)	10/56
DPU 416	AEC Regent	Strachan	H24/24R	1936	5/49	Colchester (27)	3/51
EO 7896	Guy Arab I	Park Royal	H30/26R	1942	2/51	Barrow (85)	10/55
HL 5335	Leyland TD2	Brush	L27/26R	1932	9/56	Blackwell, Earls Colne	9/57

Notes:

HD 3699 was new to Yorkshire Woollen (108)
WH 1553 was new to Bolton (54)
HL 5335 was new to West Riding (30) with a Roe H26/22D body
BEL 391 was new to Hants & Dorset (995)
DEV 479 was originally fitted with a Brush L27/26R body and was rebodied in 1949

CWM 571 was originally fitted with a Massey H29/26R body and was new as Southport (55). The ECW body came from Hants & Dorset Leyland TD1 TR 5296 and was fitted by Blackwell's in 6/51
ASD 834 was new to Western SMT (255)
XG 8203 was new to Middlesbrough (44)
AJA 118B was new to North Western Road Car Co (118)
SOE 956H was new to West Midlands PTE (3956)

CXX 379 (top left)
The pioneer double-decker in the Goldsmith fleet was a distinctively styled ex-London Transport STL class AEC. The hinged drivers door is an obvious local addition! The bus was boldly signwritten as shown in this view beside St Mary's Church in Honey Hill, Bury St Edmunds.

G R Mills collection

CWM 571 (top right)
The second hand body on this bus has a shelved scuttle below the driver's windscreen to "make good" the transfer to the TD5. Still in Honeywood's brown when seen on Angel Hill, Bury St Edmunds, with a Theobalds OWB alongside and a Longs OB at the rear. The via point blind reads Stanstead, Stanningfield, Shimpling.

G R Mills

ASD 834 (second from top right)
Still in the cream and blue livery of Wesley, Stoke Goldington, the utility Duple body has rebuilt front upper deck windows and the addition of platform doors. The only Daimler half-cab double-decker operated by Goldsmiths is also seen on Angel Hill, Bury St Edmunds, in company with a Chambers Guy Arab/Crossley and Bedford SB/Plaxton of Towler, Brandon at the rear.

G R Mills

GUF 37 (third from top right)
The halcyon days of Goldsmith double-decker operation on stage services as the Guy with austere East Lancs body leaves Angel Hill in Bury St Edmunds in March 1960 with a well loaded Saturday journey to Brettenham. Alongside is an AEC Regal III/Duple of Jolly, Norton.

G R Mills

DEV 479 (bottom right)
The only Bristol ever operated was acquired as a direct replacement for the Daimler CWA6. The 1949 ECW body was fully repainted into duo-blue and cream as seen at the usual Angel Hill venue in May 1962. Alongside is a Theobalds Bedford OB and a Simonds of Botesdale Commer/Plaxton is at the rear.

G R Mills

GPW 347 (bottom left)
The second of a pair of ex-Eastern Counties Leyland PD1/ECW ousted the Bristol from the fleet; again fully repainted into duo-blue and cream. The well-loaded bus is seen passing the Abbey Gate in August 1964 bound for Glemsford on a former Honeywood journey.

G R Mills

Hicks Bros Ltd, Fairfield Road, Braintree, Essex

Records exist as far back as 1878 of business ventures owned by the Hicks Brothers in the village of Felsted but it was not until 1914 that motorised transport replaced their horse-drawn carriers carts. In 1922, the centre of operations moved to Braintree and extra garaging was built in North Street, Dunmow, in 1928. In March 1932 the premises of the Silver End Development Co Ltd at Boars Tye Road in the village set up by Crittalls were acquired together with three service buses (two Leyland and one AEC). The original Felsted garage was sold in September 1939 to Len Woodley, formerly Hicks senior fitter, who continued to supply motor fuel, spares and repairs until June 1950 when he ventured into coach operation. An all-Bedford fleet was operated until June 1979 when the venture ceased.

The services operated by Hicks Bros during the post-war periods were:

10	Braintree - Dunmow - Bishops Stortford	daily
11	Braintree - Little Waltham - Chelmsford	daily
15	Braintree - Blackmore End - Lindsell	weekdays
16	Stebbing - Felsted - Chelmsford	Tuesdays & Fridays
17	Bishops Stortford - Takeley & Broxted circular	Thursdays & Saturdays
19	Braintree - Wethersfield	Wednesdays & Saturdays
21	Dunmow - Great Waltham - Chelmsford	daily
22	Braintree - Dunmow - Harlow - express to London	daily
29	Felsted - Willows Green - Braintree	Wednesdays
35	Braintree - Silver End - Witham	daily
49	Bishops Stortford - Great Hallingbury	Thursdays
52	Braintree - Notleys - Witham	daily

The Guy Arab IIIs were regular performers on the daily service to the "metropolis" while the array of second-hand stock was allocated to the local stage services.

Hicks Bros sold out to the British Transport Commission on 1 January 1950 and the business was placed under the management of the Eastern National Omnibus Company, all the road service and vehicle licences were transferred in 1955.

The small Dunmow garage was sold to Don Hale (Don's Coaches) in May 1950 but his coach fleet outgrew the site such that a new purpose-built garage/workshop was built on a large site at Parsonage Downs in Dunmow. The old Hicks garage was demolished and Don Hale had a modern house built on the site.

The Silver End site was closed operationally in December 1965 but subsequently served as a store before being leased to PVS (London) Ltd, precursor of Ensignbus, for vehicle sales. However, on 12 October 1974 a much-improved yard and buildings reopened as a replacement for Kelvedon depot, which had been overwhelmed with the National Travel (South East) coach fleet. Regrettably, Silver End depot finally closed on 6 August 1988 with the 12 vehicles dispersed to Braintree, Colchester and Chelmsford. The property was sold, the site cleared and houses have eliminated all evidence of bus operations. The final eradication of the Hicks empire came in April 2005 when First Essex Buses Ltd (the successors to Eastern National) sold the Fairfield Road, Braintree garage for redevelopment after 83 years of bus operation.

Livery: royal blue and yellow

1: VX 4732 (left)

The first double-decker in the Hicks fleet was a Leyland Titan TD1 with a Leyland lowheight body. Vincents of Reading carried out an extensive rebuild in 1944 which involved losing the piano-style front profile and fitting a Leyland 8.6 oil engine in place of the original petrol engine. Seen in Braintree bus park when 21 years old in 1951.

G R Mills

Double-Deckers operated 1930 - 1955

	Reg	Chassis	Body	Seats	New	In	Ex	Out
1	VX 4732	Leyland TD1	Leyland	L24/24R	1930	3/30	New	12/51
49	DPU 747	Leyland TD4	Park Royal	L27/26R	1936	5/36	New	8/52
50	WH 810	Leyland TD1	Leyland	L24/24R	1928	9/36	Bolton (46)	5/52
51	WH 1551	Leyland TD1	Leyland	L27/24R	1928	9/36	Bolton (52)	EN
52	WH 1552	Leyland TD1	Leyland	L27/24R	1929	10/36	Bolton (53)	EN
53	WH 1553	Leyland TD1	Leyland	L27/24R	1929	10/36	Bolton (54)	11/47
54	WH 1554	Leyland TD1	Leyland	L27/24R	1929	11/36	Bolton (55)	x/51
59	FHK 141	Leyland TD5	Strachans	L27/26R	1937	7/37	New	EN
62	VX 8349	Leyland TS1	Park Royal	L27/26R	1930	11/30	New	9/52
63	MW 5198	Leyland TD1	Park Royal	L27/26R	1929	5/36	Swindon (26)	6/52
65	HF 6705	Leyland TD1	Park Royal	L24/24R	1930	8/39	Harding, Birkenhead	EN
66	CK 4266	Leyland TD1	Leyland	L27/24R	1930	x/39	Ribble (816)	x/51
67	CK 4219	Leyland TD1	Leyland	L27/24R	1930	x/39	Ribble (755)	11/51
68	CK 4209	Leyland TD1	Leyland	L24/24R	1930	x/39	Ribble (745)	EN
69	CK 4270	Leyland TD1	Leyland	L24/24R	1930	1/40	Ribble (820)	12/49
70	CK 4363	Leyland TD1	Leyland	L24/24R	1930	11/40	Ribble (813)	2/52
71	HF 6703	Leyland TD1	Park Royal	L24/24R	1930	11/40	Wallasey (58)	3/52
72	HF 5881	Leyland TD1	Leyland	L27/24R	1929	7/43	Alexander (R100)	2/53
73	CH 9289	Leyland TD1	Leyland	L24/24R	1930	7/43	Baker, Warsop	x/52
74	TF 2340	Leyland TD1	Leyland	L28/24R	1930	x/45	United Welsh (563)	5/52
75	JVX 716	Guy Arab II	Weymann	L27/28R	1945	10/45	New	EN
76	KEV 217	Guy Arab II	Strachans	L27/28R	1945	7/45	New	EN
77	KEV 690	Guy Arab II	Strachans	L27/28R	1945	11/45	New	EN
78	LPU 125	Guy Arab II	Strachans	L27/26R	1947	1/47	New	EN
81	MNO 193	Leyland PD1	Leyland	L27/26R	1947	7/47	New	EN
82	MNO 194	Leyland PD1	Leyland	L27/26R	1947	7/47	New	EN
84	NEV 609	Guy Arab III	Strachans	L27/26R	1948	4/48	New	EN
85	NEV 610	Guy Arab III	Strachans	L27/26R	1948	4/48	New	EN
86	WH 4908	Leyland TD3	Strachans	L27/26R	1933	2/48	Bolton (79)	EN
90	OVW 756	Guy Arab III	Strachans	L27/28R	1949	7/49	New	EN
91	OVW 757	Guy Arab III	Strachans	L27/28R	1949	7/49	New	EN
4109	PTW 624	Guy Arab III	Strachans	L27/28R	1950	2/50	New	EN
4110	PTW 625	Guy Arab III	Strachans	L27/28R	1950	2/50	New	EN

Notes:
53 survived into preservation
62 was new with a Weymann C32F body, the Park Royal body was new in 1939
63 was new with a Leyland L27/24R body, the Park Royal body was new in 1939
65 was new to Wallasey (59) with a Davidson H27/21D body, the Park Royal body was new in 1939

71 was new with a Davidson H27/21D body, the Park Royal body was new in 1941
72 was new to Wallasey (71)
74 was originally a Leyland demonstrator
86 was new with an English Electric H28/24R body, the Strachans body was new in 1948
EN = vehicles licensed to the Eastern National Omnibus Company from 1955

(Ref: *75 years of Essex Service* by Geoff Dodson, published June 2005)

49: DPU 749 (above)
The second double-decker bought new by Hicks fleet was a Leyland Titan TD4 with a stylish Park Royal body, seen here at rest in Braintree bus park in May 1952. Alongside is an ex-Bolton Leyland TD1 with original Leyland body.

G R Mills

63: MW 5198 (below)
After the Park Royal body on the new Leyland TD4, Hicks had four Leylands (three Titan TD1 and a Tiger TS1) rebodied by Park Royal with double-deck bodies. One of these was the solitary ex-Swindon example seen in August 1951 in Braintree bus park still in original Hicks livery of blue with three yellow bands.

D S Giles

21

50: WH 810 (right)

The veteran of the fleet, this 1928 Leyland TD1 with original Leyland body, was the oldest of six ex-Bolton buses acquired by Hicks. Seen in Braintree bus park in May 1952, its last month of service with Hicks, the bus was subsequently used by a showman; 1: (VX 4732) at the rear did not fair so well as it was scrapped at the end of its Hicks service.

G R Mills

86: WH 4908 (left)

This remarkable 1933 Leyland Titan TD4 with a 1948 Strachans body unloads in Fairfield Road, Chelmsford, in June 1952. The new Eastern National Bristol KSW5G (TNO 689) is loading for London (Bow) via Brentwood and Romford in the Duke Street bus station.

G R Mills

78: LPU 125 (left)

The 1947 Strachans body shows distinct relaxed utility styling and is based on a Guy Arab II. Moore's of Kelvedon had an identical pair (LPU 611/2) which also served Braintree, the setting of this May 1952 shot.

G R Mills

91: OVW 757 (below)

This was one of the doyens of Hicks London service from new in 1949 until displaced by a batch of Bristol KSW5G/ECW with platform doors in 1953. The distinctive front rake of the Strachans body can be clearly seen in this July 1952 view in Braintree bus park. The Guy Arab III (5LW) chassis was later used by Moore Bros of Kelvedon, rebodied by Massey and reregistered JTW 447.

G R Mills

Ipswich Coach Co Ltd, Pine Trees, Elton Park, Hadleigh Road, Ipswich, Suffolk

Entrepreneurial enthusiast David Boughton and keen busman Ron Abbot established Ipswich Coach Co in May 1970 with a pair of ex-Western National Bristol LS6G/ECW coaches. Gaining a school contract added a further Bristol LS6B/ECW bus to the fleet. A year later, advancement into double-deck operation meant forsaking the sanctuary of a yard in an upmarket housing area of Ipswich for a parking area in a carved out chalk pit at the rear of a garage between Ipswich and Needham Market (then on the A45 trunk road, now the B1113). Three more Bristol LS/ECW were acquired from Hedingham Omnibuses and a pair of Grey-Green group Leyland Leopard/Harrington coaches and two ex London Transport AEC Regal IV RF types were added to the fleet in 1972. Most were attired in the attractive white, grey and orange livery.

When Eastern Counties withdrew service 231 (Ipswich - Grundisburgh - Woodbridge) in May 1972 the opportunity was taken to venture into regular bus workings, with the added incentive of generous Department of Transport grants for new vehicles bought for stage services. Accordingly, a new Ford R192 with Plaxton bodywork fitted with the requisite folding doors was purchased. An ex-Bournemouth Leyland Tiger Cub and an ex-Ipswich AEC Regal IV also performed journeys on the service. Another interesting acquisition was an ex-Western Welsh Albion Nimbus acquired from A C Aldis of Felixstowe Ferry when the latter's long established weekday service into Felixstowe passed to Eastern Counties in 1972.

The ICC enterprise ceased in December 1974 with five of the vehicles and the stage service passing to JDW Transport in Ipswich. David Boughton went on to form a number of other businesses: Stanlake Passenger Transport Co Ltd; Felixstowe Omnibuses Ltd, which traded as Blue Bus Services; and Rallybeam Ltd, which also traded as Blue Bus Services and was based initially at Debach and later at Framlingham. An interesting aspect of this latter operation was a brave seafront service at Felixstowe in 1990 followed by an even more ambitious venture operating three Leyland Atlantean open-toppers between Paignton and Torquay in 1994-1997, trading as Bulleys Bus Service, in direct competition with a similar service operated by Stagecoach.

Livery: white and grey with orange wheels

Double-Deckers operated 1971 - 1974

	Reg	Chassis	Body	Seats	New	In	Ex	Out
5	SFV 412	Leyland PDR1/1	Weymann	H34/16F	1960	2/71	Ribble (16)	1/72
8	PFN 844	AEC Regent V	Park Royal	H40/32F	1959	9/71	East Kent	9/72
18	410 COR	Dennis Loline III	Alexander	H39/29F	1961	8/72	Aldershot & District (410)	5/73

PFN 844 (left)

One of a unique batch of 40 delivered to East Kent in 1959 (apart from an ex-demo model with Liverpool Corporation), PFN 844 is seen at the Needham Market operating centre in September 1971 when freshly repainted into ICC's attractive white and grey livery. The bus later saw service with Continental Pioneer, Richmond and even later with Richardson of Helston, Cornwall.

G R Mills

SFV 412 (right)

Originally one of the famed "Gay Hostess" batch of 37 built in 1959-61 for Ribble (and its associated W C Standerwick and Scout Motor Services fleets) for the Lancashire - Birmingham - London express services. The body's stylish lines are evident in this December 1971 view at the Needham Market depot. The vehicle was later operated by the Oak Hill Youth Club at Caterham.

G R Mills

W A Jolly, the Garage, Norton, Suffolk

A typical rural Suffolk operator established in the late twenties such that by 1932 a new Dennis Dart (normal control and petrol engined - far removed from the modern model bearing the same type name) was purchased. Another classic added in 1937 was a new half-cab Leyland Cub/Duple to replace an ex-Corona Morris Director/Duple. For the next two decades, all coaches bought new and used had Hendon built coachwork. These included a new Leyland Tiger PS1 and AEC Regal III and a pair of used Albion Valkyries.

In the early post-war years, three services were operated:

Wyverstone - Bury St Edmunds	Daily
Norton - Ipswich	Tuesdays
Norton - Stowmarket	Thursdays

The patronage on the Bury service on Wednesdays (market days) and Saturdays required duplication which prompted the purchase of the first double-decker. Guided by the characteristic E Jack Mulley of Ixworth, the nearest neighbouring operator, a visit to W North's yards in Leeds in 1954 resulted in three ex-London STL class buses moving to Suffolk. The Jolly choice was a "Tunnel" type with a specially shaped roof to negotiate the Blackwall and Rotherhithe tunnels under the Thames. Mulley had a similar model and a more standard example, the latter achieving fame when fully restored by the London Bus Preservation Trust at Cobham, Surrey, in 2000.

A slight retrenchment occurred in 1958 when an AEC Reliance/Burlingham Seagull was acquired and a pair of Bedford OBs were sold. One of the latter had a Mulliner bus body and was acquired by Mulley's, named "Jolly Roger" and given Corona Coaches fleetnames following that company's demise in 1959, to work on the Sudbury town service. The Jolly family retired from the bus business in June 1964 and sold the fleet to Mulley's. The dutch barn type garage was used by Mulley's to break up a batch of ex-Great Yarmouth Leyland PD1/Massey double-deckers but the site was subsequently sold for housing

Livery: cream, red and maroon

Double-Deckers operated 1954 - 1962

Reg	Chassis	Body	Seats	New	In	Ex	Out
DLU 235	AEC Regent	LPTB	H30/25R	1937	5/54	London Transport (STL1867)	5/59
ACK831	Guy Arab II	Roe	L27/26R	1944	9/56	Ribble (2441)	12/62

DLU 235 (right)

A classic bus departs Angel Hill, Bury St Edmunds, on a market day in August 1956, passing Long's of Glemsford GV 9866, a Bedford OB/Duple, with one of Theobalds Bedford OWBs still loading in the background. Prior to the opening of the new bus station in St Andrews Street North in April 1996, all the independents used the location for parking and departures producing a plethora of colours and types.

G R Mills

ACK 831 (below)

Whereas the STL had been fully repainted, the Guy was operated in "as acquired" livery, with even the Ribble fleet number intact, and is seen here in March 1960 departing Norton village bound for Bury St Edmunds. The Roe body was rebuilt by Bond of Wythenshawe in 1951. Note the SBG style destination box also specified by Ribble.

G R Mills

A E Letch, Wethersfield Road, Sible Hedingham, Essex

Aubrey Letch started in the motor business after demobilisation from World War I. His first new vehicle was a 1920 Buick with a 1916 truck body which also served as a 14-seat bus on market days, running to Braintree on Wednesdays and Sudbury on Thursdays. An early association was established with Syd Blackwell at Earls Colne, a similar ex-serviceman who pioneered bus services, for complete vehicles and spares, as well as engineering facilities.

By the early post-war years, the following services were operated:

Sible Hedingham - Braintree	Wednesdays & Saturdays
Great Yeldham - Braintree	Mondays to Saturdays
Sible Hedingham - Sudbury	Thursdays & Saturdays

The double-decker was the regular allocation on the weekday service to Braintree whilst either one of a pair of ex-West Yorkshire Leyland Tiger TS3 buses normally shared the Sudbury route before being displaced by a pair of ex-Metropolitan Police Bedford OBs with Mulliner bus bodies. A pair of interesting coaches was acquired in the late 40s, these being a new Guy Vixen with a rare Withnell body and a 1933 Leyland Titanic with a 1938 Harrington body. The latter's chassis had been new to the City Coach Co as TS2 with a Dodson H34/28R body.

In June 1960 the eight-vehicle business, which included two double-deckers, was acquired by D R MacGregor and formed the basis of Hedingham & District Omnibuses. As a lasting token of the founder of the operations, every vehicle acquired, both new and used, has an "L" prefix to the fleetnumber. All the ex-Letch stock was sold by May 1963.

Livery: blue and cream
             duo brown after the acquisition of the sole coach of Meggs, Halstead in September 1955

Double-Deckers operated 1945 - 1960

Reg	Chassis	Body	Seats	New	In	Ex	Out
JY 3664	Leyland TD3	Leyland	L24/24R	1934	8/45	Plymouth (11)	8/51
UF 5651	Leyland TD1	Leyland	L24/24R	1930	4/50	Southdown (851)	3/53
LJ 9405	Leyland TD3	Brush	L27/26R	1934	6/51	Hants & Dorset	9/58
DJY 966	Crossley DD42/5	Crossley	L27/26R	1948	7/58	Plymouth (336)	6/60
DJY 961	Crossley DD42/5	Crossley	L27/26R	1948	12/59	Cheek, Harrow	6/60

Note - DJY 961 was new to Plymouth (331)

(Ref: *25 years of Public Service Hedingham Omnibuses 1960-1985* by G R Mills, published by Hedingham & District Omnibuses Ltd and *30 years of Public Hedingham Omnibuses 1985-1990* by G R Mills, published by Hedingham & District Omnibuses Ltd)

DJY 961

The last double-decker purchased by Letch was the second all-Crossley to join the fleet. Ex-Plymouth stock was popular in many East Anglian fleets and even more beyond. Letch had a previous expatriate from the same Devon source, an all-Leyland double-decker, in the days when the fleet livery was blue. DJY 961 is seen here in Sudbury, Station Road on layover on a market day in June 1960. In the following month, the bus was acquired by Hedingham Omnibuses and given fleet number L20. When repainted, ivory replaced the light brown and mid-blue the dark brown, although this was extended on to the bonnet cover and the band over the lower deck windows.

G R Mills

Moore Bros (Kelvedon) Ltd, Roslyn Garage, High Street

After 148 years of public service, there was little doubt that the claim by Moore Bros (Kelvedon) Ltd that they were the oldest established operators of passenger transport in the Eastern Traffic Area (all of Norfolk, Suffolk and Cambridgeshire, most of Essex and part of Bedfordshire) was justly true. They also boasted that there had never been a strike.

Following WW1, when motorisation was replacing horse drawn vehicles, Moore's had tried solid-tyred, open-top double-deckers but these were ousted by Chevrolet, GMC and REO saloons which provided all the services in the late 20s and early 30s. It was not until late in 1937 and early 1938 that the first intake of double-deckers was completed which was to spearhead the breed in the fleet continuously. Lowbridge vehicles were essential to the operations in order to pass under the railway bridges in Station Road Kelvedon and Duke Street, Chelmsford. The pioneer 'deckers were ex City of Oxford where a similar problem existed with a low bridge adjacent to the main railway station.

Apart from the allocation by the Ministry of War Transport of a Bristol K5G, all further new and used double-deckers were Guys, fitted with the 5-cylinder Gardner 5LW engine on which the fleet standardised. Furthermore there were four new and four second-hand Arab III/Strachan coaches, which were similarly powered. An interesting feature of the Moore's double-deck fleet was the various rebodyings undertaken between 1943 and 1960: The first three petrol engined AECs received utility bodies in place of the original Hall Lewis coachwork; whilst later years saw the utility bodies on 4 Guy Arabs replaced with new Strachan products. Five years on, 3 later Strachans bodied Arabs received stylish Massey coachwork, two utilised ex Hicks Bros chassis.

The public were conveyed by this fine fleet on many main road routes including:
Colchester - Witham - Chelmsford
Colchester - Coggeshall - Braintree
Colchester - Tiptree - Tolleshunt Knights
Colchester - Tiptree (Ship)
Chelmsford - Hatfield Peverel - Maldon.

The freehold property and 43 vehicles (including 26 Guy double-deckers and 12 Arab saloons) passed to the Eastern National Omnibus Co after 2 February 1963. The premises were used exclusively by Eastern National until the autumn of 1973 when the East Anglian base of National Travel (South East) was set up at Kelvedon. Eastern National left in October 1974, transferring operations to the Silver End premises inherited from Hicks. In October 1978, Eastern National re-established coach operations, National Travel (South East) was disbanded and the Kelvedon depot closed. The next occupant was Geoff Whybrow, trading as Kelvedon Coaches, until March 1983 when the business failed and the fleet and equipment was auctioned. The site was subsequently purchased by a developer and split into units, the principal occupier of the workshop area being Hedingham Omnibuses from March 1986. The offices, originally built in 1879 as Moore's Temperance Hotel, still stand in Kelvedon High Street, structurally unaltered apart from the windows. The main entrance to the left (when viewed from the front) was blocked in NTSE days and a new wide access was created to the right of the office buildings. In 1975, Eastern National withdrew the last of the Guys so the link with Moore Bros was lost. Fortunately, one of the most attractive examples, 373 WPU, still exists in preservation at the Castle Point Bus Museum on Canvey Island, housed in a former Eastern National depot.

Livery: mid green and cream

WL 9062

The pioneer double-deckers which took the Moore's fleet into the post WWII years were a trio of petrol-engined AEC Regents. Moore's had all three rebodied as shown by this November 1953 view in St Johns Street bus station, Colchester. The leading bus has a Willowbrook utility body, whilst WL 9068 at the rear was an NCB utility product.

G R Mills

Double-Deckers operated 1946 - 1963

Reg	Chassis	Body	Seats	New	In	Ex	Out
WL 9062	AEC Regent	Willowbrook	L27/26R	1930	12/37	Oxford (G131)	10/55
WL 9063	AEC Regent	Willowbrook	L27/26R	1930	12/37	Oxford (G137)	2/55
WL 9068	AEC Regent	NCB	L27/26R	1930	6/38	Oxford (G132)	10/55
VH 4875	Leyland TD2	Leyland	L24/24R	1933	x/40	Hanson, Huddersfield (60)	10/46
UF 6468	Leyland TD1	Leyland	L24/24R	1930	x/40	Southdown (868)	10/46
WN 4762	AEC Regent	Brush	L25/26R	1932	12/41	South Wales (262	5/47
JPU 640	Bristol K5G	Duple	L27/28R	1942	7/42	New	5/58
JTW 447	Guy Arab I	Brush	L27/28R	1943	5/43	New	EN
JVW 999	Guy Arab II	Roe	L27/28R	1944	8/44	New	EN
JVX 223	Guy Arab II	Strachans	L27/28R	1945	4/45	New	9/58
JVX 555	Guy Arab II	Strachans	L27/28R	1945	7/45	New	8/61 (EN)
JVX 556	Guy Arab II	Strachans	L27/28R	1945	7/45	New	EN
JVX 557	Guy Arab II	Strachans	L27/28R	1945	8/45	New	EN
JVX 558	Guy Arab II	Strachans	L27/28R	1945	9/45	New	EN
LPU 611	Guy Arab III	Strachans	L27/28R	1947	3/47	New	EN
LPU 612	Guy Arab III	Strachans	L27/28R	1947	3/47	New	EN
ONO 537	Guy Arab III	Strachans	L27/28R	1949	7/49	New	EN
ONO 538	Guy Arab III	Strachans	L27/28R	1949	7/49	New	EN
GYL 983	Guy Arab II	Weymann	L27/28R	1945	8/51	Birch Bros (K103)	EN
GYL 984	Guy Arab II	Weymann	L27/28R	1945	9/51	Birch Bros (K104)	EN
GYL 981	Guy Arab II	Weymann	L27/28R	1945	1/52	Birch Bros (K101)	EN
GYL 982	Guy Arab II	Weymann	L27/28R	1945	4/52	Birch Bros (K102)	EN
YEV 263	Guy Arab IV	Strachans	L28/28R	1954	3/54	New	EN
52 DHK	Guy Arab IV	Strachans	L28/28R	1955	7/55	New	EN
53 DHK	Guy Arab IV	Strachans	L28/28R	1955	7/55	New	EN
2834 F	Guy Arab IV	NCME	L31/32R	1957	7/57	New	EN
2835 F	Guy Arab IV	NCME	L31/32R	1957	7/57	New	EN
8935 NO	Guy Arab IV	Massey	L34/33R	1958	9/58	New	EN
8936 NO	Guy Arab IV	Massey	L34/33R	1959	10/58	New	EN
19 PVX	Guy Arab IV	Massey	L34/33R	1959	7/59	New	EN
20 PVX	Guy Arab IV	Massey	L34/33R	1959	7/59	New	EN
372 WPU	Guy Arab IV	Massey	L34/33R	1961	5/61	New	EN
373 WPU	Guy Arab IV	Massey	L34/33R	1961	5/61	New	EN

Vehicles ordered by Moore's:
581 AOO and 582 AOO (Guy Arab IV/Massey L34/33R) were delivered to Eastern National in March 1963

Vehicles acquired for spares:

EO 7896	Guy Arab I	Strachans	L27/28R	1942	10/55	Honeywood, Stanstead	
OVW 756	Guy Arab III	Strachans	L27/28R	1949	8/59	Eastern National (1191)	
OVW 757	Guy Arab III	Strachans	L27/28R	1949	8/59	Eastern National (1192)	

Notes:
WL 9063/2/8 originally had Hall Lewis L24/24R bodies and were rebodied in 1943/4/5
JTW 447 was rebodied Massey L29/28R in 10/60 using the chassis frame from OVW 757
JVW 999 was rebodied Massey L29/28R in 5/60 using the chassis frame from OVW 756
LPU 611 was rebodied Massey L29/28R in 4/60

GYL 981-983 were rebodied Strachans L28/28R in 1954
GYL 984 was rebodied Strachans L28/28R in 2/55
EO 7896 was new to Barrow (85)
OVW 756 and OVW 757 were new to Hicks, Braintree
373 WPU survived into preservation
EN = vehicles passed to the Eastern National Omnibus Company in February 1963

(Ref: *Buses Illustrated 132*, March 1966, and *Classic Bus 64*, April/May 2003)

373 WPU

Epitomising the appalling weather experienced during the last months of Moore's operations, this January 1963 view shows the newest Guy Arab IV at Marks Tey roundabout. The bus is en-route from Colchester and has reached the junction where the A120 to Braintree meets the main A12 to Chelmsford. Fortunately this splendid Massey bodied bus has been saved for preservation and has appeared at many local rallies in the ensuing years.

G R Mills

JTW 447 (top right)

A one off in the Moore's fleet as the only Guy Arab I and the only Brush utility body and the only one of the wartime double-deckers to have the cream band below the drivers cab windscreen. The front upper-deck windows had been set in rubber mouldings as shown in this May 1959 view at St Johns Street bus station in Colchester.   *G R Mills*

JVX 557 (top left)

This was another Arab to receive the modified front upper-deck windows, but to a Strachans utility body (one of five with Moore's). Seen leaving Colchester bus station via the East Hill exit in July 1962.

G R Mills

LPU 611 (centre right)

Further rebodying of Guy Arab chassis was undertaken in 1960, but with Massey Bros bodies, which re-entered service after four new Massey bodied Guy Arab IVs had joined the fleet. The translucent roof panels can be clearly seen in this view beside the forge in West End Road at the Tiptree (Ship) terminus.

G R Mills

GYL 984 (centre left)

Moore's association with Strachans continued through to 1954 when four ex-Birch Bros 7'6" Arab II chassis were rebodied with stylish 8ft wide bodies. One is seen at the Regal cinema in Crouch Street, Colchester, during January 1963.

G R Mills

LPU 612 (bottom right)

The twin to LPU 611 remained as built and is seen here in the layover area of Colchester's Queen Street bus station in August 19672 with KGT 380, a Guy Arab/Strachans alongside. LPU 611 survived into Eastern National ownership, receiving a full repaint which eliminated the lower cream waist band and working at Clacton in the summer of 1963 on the seasonal services to the many caravan parks.

G R Mills

Morley's Grey Coaches Ltd, Blenheim Garage, West Row, Suffolk

The close proximity to the huge RAF Mildenhall airbase might lead the uninitiated to assume that the premises were named after the WW2 Bristol Blenheim night-fighter but this was not so as Walter Morley established his coach business on the site six years before the MoD fence was erected, naming his property after the apple trees that were lost in order to build his garages. The outbreak of war greatly increased the number of personnel at the base and in consequence Morley's work loadings multiplied to warrant double-deck operation. The Ministry of War Transport allocated both a new Bedford OWB bus and a brand new utility Daimler double-decker which ousted the pioneer petrol-engined Leyland TD1. However second hand makes and models were to feature in the fleet for some 31 years.

The post war saloons varied from new Dennis Lancets, Maudslay Marathon IIIs and AEC Regal IIIs to 7 ex-Western SMT Bedford OWB and 10 pre-war AEC Regal and Regent chassis (ex Valliant and City of Oxford) which were rebodied as coaches for Morley's. A London service was operated 3 days a week for many years and there were also market day runs to Bury St Edmunds (ceased in 1957) and Ely (which survived until 1964).

After 30 years continuously providing transfers for the USAF at Mildenhall airbase, the work was lost in November 1983. School contracts for Suffolk County Council also reduced from 15 to 4 at this time and only a third of the 190 tours envisaged materialised, factors that crippled the company. The receivers were called in on 12 July 1985 and the operators' licence was revoked on 6 August. The fleet was duly auctioned off on 20 September ending Morley's Grey occupation of the site after nearly 60 years. Two of the coaches remained in the village with B J Taylor-Balls, D Boreham and R Isaacson, a partnership with the former involved in haulage. Trading as West Row Coach Services they were initially based at the former Morley premises. After November 1992 the business was owned by the Taylor-Balls only and a limited company was formed in January 2003 operating from Mildenhall Road in the village. The Blenheim garage buildings were demolished and the site was developed for some 24 houses.

Livery: grey and maroon

Double-Deckers operated 1939 - 1970

Reg	Chassis	Body	Seats	New	In	Ex	Out
UF 5538	Leyland TD1	Leyland	L24/24R	1929	11/39	Long, Glemsford	8/43
TR 6211	Leyland TD1	Leyland	L24/24R	1929	11/42	Hants & Dorset (E262)	3/43
GO 1526	Leyland TD1	Birch	H30/26RO	1931	8/43	Valliant, London W5	1/47
MY 1140	Leyland TD1	Dodson	H28/26RO	1929	8/43	Valliant, London W5	1/47
GV 8898	Daimler CWA6	Duple	L27/28R	1943	8/43	New	5/61
GC 7493	Leyland TD1	Dodson	H28/26RO	1930	6/45	Martin, Windsor	12/47
GE 7214	Leyland TD1	Croft	L31/24R	1930	5/46	Paisley & District (276)	6/50
GE 7215	Leyland TD1	Croft	L31/24R	1930	5/46	Paisley & District (277)	6/50
AOP 776	Daimler COG5	BRCW	H30/24R	1935	8/48	Birmingham (776)	7/51
MV 1518	AEC Regent	Brush	H31/25R	1931	3/49	Lancaster (4)	1/54
BWA 832	AEC Regent	Weymann	H30/26R	1935	4/50	Sheffield (232)	7/54
SN 9717	Daimler CWA6	Brush	H30/26R	1944	8/50	Clyde Coast, Ardrossan	11/56
CVP 134	AEC Regent	Metro-Cammell	H30/24R	1937	4/51	Jones, Kenfig Hill	3/56
FOP 390	Daimler CWA6	Park Royal	H30/26R	1945	4/51	Birmingham (1390)	3/60
OF 3988	AEC Regent	Brush	H30/21R	1930	1/52	Birmingham (356)	12/56
KGK 777	AEC Regent III	Cravens	H30/26R	1949	11/56	London Transport (RT1518)	11/70
CS 8057	Leyland TD5	Leyland	H30/26R	1939	3/57	Western SMT (D157)	2/61

Notes:
UF 5538 was new to Southdown (838)
GO 1526 was new to Birch Bros, Kentish Town (B37), later London Transport (TD82)
MY 1140 was new to Pioneer, London W12, later London Transport (L108)

GC 7493 was new to Nelson, London E4, later London Transport (L50)
GE 7214/5 were new to Glasgow (182/3)
MV 1518 was new as an AEC demonstrator
CVP 134 was new to Birmingham (1034)

(Ref: *Buses 370*, January 1986)

CS 8057

The last double-decker added to the Morley fleet was a pre-war Leyland then 18 years old, although the body, which had been extensively rebuilt by ECW, belies the true age of the bus. Beside the Leyland is GV 8898, a Daimler CWA6/Duple which was new to Morley's, allocated on account of the considerable numbers of military personnel conveyed during WWII. The pair of veterans are seen in December 1960 at the West Row premises.

G R Mills

W Norfolk & Sons, Mill Street, Nayland, Suffolk

With the demise of Moore Bros of Kelvedon in February 1963, Norfolk's gained the title of Britain's oldest independent bus operator. A major milestone was reached in January 1915, when the first motorised bus took 45 minutes to complete the 6-mile journey to Colchester. In the 1920s open-topped double-deckers with rear open staircases and solid tyres were operated into Colchester through to the early 30s. A period of running an all saloon fleet followed until 1938 when a used double-decker of a much more advanced design became available on pneumatic tyres.

Throughout the ensuing war years there was a consistent need for double-deck capacity workings but from 1956 to 1976 only one double-decker was operated, this being employed on the main road service from Stoke-by-Nayland to Colchester via Nayland and Great Horkesley.

Under Howard Norfolk's (the fifth generation) management, a unique purchase was made when five consecutively registered double-deckers entered the fleet; specially selected for the "as acquired" livery was green and cream, which thus did not require a repaint! The five were the mainstay of the double-deck fleet, the only other one being a novelty open-top AEC Renown used on private hire work and driver training which had replaced an Albion Lowlander employed on the latter duties.

When Hedingham Omnibuses acquired the operations and vehicles on 26 April 1991, no premises were involved in the takeover; the house/office and workshop remained in Norfolk ownership. The latter acted as a store for a pair of Austin CXB with Mann Egerton bodies and a Bedford SB8/Duple. Two other locations in the village used by Norfolk's are no longer accessible to large vehicles: The Top Shed in Bear Street is now occupied by a large house and the "Perry" yard at the main cross roads in Nayland is the site of a pair of executive houses. Hedingham Omnibuses used this location until August 1993 when the vehicles transferred to Sudbury. Within 5¼ years, all the ex-Norfolk stock had been sold by Hedingham whilst the last proprietor, Howard, emigrated to Sydney, Australia, in January 1996, severing Nayland's link with over 150 years of bus operation.

Livery: duo green and cream

Double-Deckers operated 1938 - 1991

Reg	Chassis	Body	Seats	New	In	Ex	Out
MW 4146	Leyland TD1	Leyland	L24/24R	1929	6/38	Blackwell, Earls Colne	7/52
VO 7884	AEC Renown	Strachan	H36/30R	1932	8/44	Burwell & District	7/51
KJ 1912	Leyland TD1	Leyland	H24/24R	1931	5/46	Burwell & District	6/53
BWA 831	AEC Regent	Weymann	H30/26R	1935	7/49	Sheffield (231)	6/55
FOF 296	Leyland TD6c	Leyland	H28/24R	1939	9/54	Lansdowne, London E11	12/62
BDJ 70	AEC Regent III	Park Royal	H30/26R	1950	1/63	St Helens (D70)	12/66
TWL 928	AEC Regent III	Park Royal	H30/26R	1953	11/66	Oxford (928)	6/72
399 COR	Dennis Loline III	Alexander	H39/29F	1961	4/72	Aldershot & District (399)	3/76
SBN 767	AEC Regent V	MCW	H40/32F	1961	1/76	Gtr Manchester PTE (6667)	7/81
64 RTO	Daimler CRG6LX	NCME	H44/33F	1963	10/76	Nottingham (64)	11/82
69 RTO	Daimler CRG6LX	NCME	H44/33F	1963	12/77	Nottingham (69)	8/82
DEB 484C	Daimler CRG6LX	Willowbrook	H43/32F	1965	7/79	Burwell & District	8/81
SOE 941H	Daimler CRG6LX-33	Park Royal	H47/33D	1969	10/80	Partridge, Hadleigh	12/84
SOE 913H	Daimler CRG6LX-33	Park Royal	H47/33D	1969	4/81	West Midlands PTE (3913)	5/90
301 XRA	Daimler CRG6LX	Weymann	H44/33F	1962	7/81	Chesterfield (301)	2/84
SOE 978H	Daimler CRG6LX-33	Park Royal	H47/33D	1969	9/82	Partridge, Hadleigh	5/90
PRG 137J	Daimler CRG6LX-33	Alexander	H48/32D	1971	12/82	Partridge, Hadleigh	1/90
NNB 598H	Daimler CRG6LXB-33	Park Royal	H47/35F	1970	1/84	Gtr Manchester PTE (2139)	5/90
NRD 61M	Bristol VRT/LL2/6LX	NCME	H47/29D	1973	3/84	Reading (61)	4/90
NRD 54M	Bristol VRT/LL2/6LX	NCME	H47/29D	1974	4/84	Reading (54)	11/89
NNB 589H	Daimler CRG6LXB-33	Park Royal	H47/28D	1970	12/84	Gtr Manchester PTE (2130)	10/90
BRR 85C	Albion LR3	NCME	H41/33F	1965	1/86	Preservation	8/89
PRG 138J	Daimler CRG6LX	Alexander	H48/32F	1971	9/86	Cutting, Brockley	4/88
DAU 379C	AEC Renown	Weymann	O40/30F	1965	5/89	Glemsford Emeralds	4/91
PRG 126J	Daimler CRG6LX	Alexander	H48/37F	1971	1/90	Tally Ho!, Kingsbridge	4/91
OJD 199R	Leyland Fleetline	MCW	H44/33F	1976	2/90	Graham, Paisley (D1)	9/90
CBV 305S	Leyland AN68A/2R	East Lancs	H50/36F	1977	5/90	Blackpool (305)	4/91
CBV 306S	Leyland AN68A/2R	East Lancs	H50/36F	1977	5/90	Blackpool (306)	4/91
CBV 307S	Leyland AN68A/2R	East Lancs	H50/36F	1977	5/90	Blackpool (307)	4/91
CBV 308S	Leyland AN68A/2R	East Lancs	H50/36F	1977	5/90	Blackpool (308)	4/91
CBV 309S	Leyland AN68A/2R	East Lancs	H50/36F	1977	5/90	Blackpool (309)	4/91

Notes:
MW 4146 was new to Swindon (15)
VO 7884 was new to Ebor Bus Co, Mansfield (6) and then passed to Western SMT
KJ 1912 was new to Maidstone & District (218), then London Transport (TD136B)
FOF 296 was new to Birmingham (1296)
SBN 767 was new to Bolton (67)

SOE 940/78H were new to West Midlands PTE (3941/78)
PRG 126/37/8J were new to Aberdeen (126/37/8)
BRR 85C was new to South Notts, Gotham (85)
DAU 379C was new to Nottingham (379) and then passed to Theobald, Long Melford.
OJD 199R was new to London transport (DMS2199)
TWL 928 and NNB 589/98H survived into preservation

(Ref: *Buses Extra 40* April/May 1986; *Buses Extra 74* December/January 1991/92; *Norfolk's, Nayland* by Geoff Mills, published 1995 by W Norfolk & Sons Ltd, Nayland)

Norfolk's pre-war double-deckers

VO 7884
Originally one of two AEC Renowns supplied to the Ebor Bus Co of Mansfield in 1932, the pair passed to Western SMT in 1936 before VO 7884 came into the well-known Burwell & District fleet in Cambridgeshire. The impressive 66-seater is seen in the St Johns Street bus station in Colchester in 1949.

Ralph Eves

KJ 1912
This petrol-engined Leyland TD1 started life with Maidstone & District in 1931, only to pass to London Transport (Country Area) in July 1933 before acquisition by Burwell & District in 1941 and is seen here in St Johns Street bus station in Colchester in 1950 on the Wednesday and Saturday service to Boxted. Double-deckers rarely appeared on this service, operated in direct competition with Went's of Boxted, after the TD1 was withdrawn in 1953.

G R Mills collection

BWA 831
The first diesel-engined double-decker in the Norfolk's fleet became the regular performer on the main road service from Stoke-by-Nayland to Colchester on Mondays to Saturdays and is seen here in St Johns Street bus station, on the regular stand, surrounded by Eastern National stock, a Bristol K alongside and a Bristol L behind.

John Carman

FOF 296
For twenty years from 1956 to 1976, Norfolk's only operated one double-decker. The first of these was this 1939 Leyland TD6c with distinctive Birmingham style Leyland body which operated the "main road" for eight years. The stalwart is seen at the Angel, Stoke-by-Nayland crossroads in September 1962, three months before final withdrawal.

G R Mills

Norfolk's front-engined double-deckers

BDJ 70 (top right)
Only the registration number reveals the true identity of what appears to be an ex-London Transport RT (as there were over 4,560 look-alikes) but the Norfolk's bus was one of 40 supplied to St Helens. Seen turning at Blundens Estate, Stoke-by-Nayland, in November 1966. *G R Mills*

TWL 928 (second from top right)
The same chassis/body combination as the "RT", but three years newer, this AEC Regent III/Park Royal was acquired from the well respected City of Oxford fleet. Seen turning at Harpers Estate, Nayland, in January 1967, smartly attired in the duo-green and cream livery. *G R Mills*

399 COR (third from top right)
The replacement for the Regent III was the first front-entrance double-decker to join the fleet. Acquired in Aldershot & District duo-green, the only changes made were cream wheels and the addition of fleetnames. The Dennis Loline also pioneered the Gardner engine in the double-deck fleet, 14 others following from 1976. Seen in Horkesley Road, Nayland in February 1976. *G R Mills*

SBN 767 (bottom right)
SBN was an appropriate registration as the Regent V was to terminate at Stoke-By-Nayland every weekday for five years! Seen outside the White Hart Hotel in Nayland in February 1976 freshly repainted into duo-green and cream, this was to be the last crew operated double-decker in Norfolk's fleet. *G R Mills*

BRR 85C (top left)
Five years after the Regent V was sold, the need arose for a manual gearbox double-decker to train potential drivers. The Albion Lowlander (boldly badged Leyland) filled this requirement admirably and is seen in Stoke-by-Nayland in March 1986 still in South Notts distinctive blue livery. *G R Mills*

DAU 379C (bottom left)
A rare conversion was completed by Norfolk's on the one-time Theobalds AEC Renown, planned to perform driver training, special private hires and occasional tree cutting duties. The smartly turned out bus is seen at Colchester Castle Gates, Cowdray Crescent in September 1989. Still in the fleet when Hedingham took over in April 1991, it found little use before onward sale to Partridge of Hadleigh. *G R Mills*

Norfolk's rear-engined double-deckers

64/69 RTO (top left)
The ex-Nottingham Fleetlines available from Ensignbus suited Norfolk's well; the green and cream livery did not need a repaint and the Gardner power units were ideal. Ironically both these buses were withdrawn some seven years before a 2 year newer ex Nottingham bus was acquired in the shape of an AEC Renown!

G R Mills

SOE 913/941/978H (second from top left)
Increased school contracts gained prompted the need to acquire three "Jumbos" sourced via Partridge of Hadleigh. All three received duo-green below the waist while 913 retained the WMPTE sandpaper roof and 941/978 had two variants of the Partridge caramel applications. The trio is lined up on Sheepen Road car park in March 1984.

G R Mills

NRD 61/54M (third from top left)
To add to the WMPTE "whoppers", a pair of ex-Reading VRT/ Northern Counties, which had been signwritten "Jumbos" when new, was acquired. This addition meant that six of Norfolk's double-deckers (then including PRG137J illustrated below) were dual-door, a layout allowed on Suffolk CC contracts but not permitted on Essex CC work. The pair is seen in "The Perry" yard in Nayland in April 1986.

G R Mills

PRG 137J (top right)
A useful source of revenue was gained by allowing an advertiser the entire bus as a mobile hoarding. Freshly attired in brown and orange, with only the fleetname on a small green panel, 137 is seen on Anchor Bridge, Nayland, in March 1986, prior to a heavy downpour.

G R Mills

NNB 598H (middle right)
The influx of dual door double-deckers abated when a pair of ex-Manchester standards (ie latter day Mancunians) was acquired with 598 rebuilt as shown on Sheepen Road car park in March 1984. 589, basically acquired for spares, was put into service, still dual-door, but with the windscreen reduced to suit a standard VRT.

G R Mills

CBV 305-9S (bottom right)
The only time Norfolk's bought five consecutively registered double-deckers was from Blackpool, swayed by the cream and green livery, excellent high capacity seating and the single door. The quintet is seen on Sheepen Road car park in July 1990. A year later all five passed to Hedingham Omnibuses and survived a further five years in the area before being ousted by Bristol VRTs.

G R Mills

T M Smith (t/a Y C Travel), 10 Ber Street, Norwich, Norfolk
Fleetname: Norfolk Bluebird

After the collapse of the Red Car service in August 1981, the psv scene in Norwich was somewhat unstable. JDW of Ipswich took on the coaching duties but only survived until December 1981 only to endure the same fate. A new enterprise came on the scene in January 1983 with eight vehicles transferred from the fleet of Young's Coaches of Rampton (hence the Y C Travel trading name). The intake included 3 double-deckers, 4 Bedfords and a DAF/Plaxton as the front line coach.

An ambitious stage service, from Frettenham, where a school contract terminated, via Norwich to Great Yarmouth was operated on Wednesdays and Saturdays with a double-decker but outstanding was the take over of Norwich City services 550/552 surrendered by Eastern Counties from 3 January 1984. These served the Heartsease Estate and the University residences and were the first instance of independent operation of Norwich City services for some 60 years. Any of the ex-London DMS types were regular performers on these workings.

The innovative proprietor tried some enterprising express services provided by coaches, including Cromer to Clacton (seasonal), and Norwich to London (Kings Cross), a daily service named "The Londoner". However all operations ceased in April 1986 when two single deck vehicles and the Ber Street office facility passed to A W Easton of The Grange, Brandiston; but none of the service workings were perpetuated.

Livery: duo blue and cream

Double-Deckers operated 1983 - 1986

Reg	Chassis	Body	Seats	New	In	Ex	Out
MLK 556L	Daimler CRL6	Park Royal	H45/28D	1973	1/83	Young, Rampton	9/83
THM 712M	Daimler CRL6	MCW	H44/27D	1974	1/83	Young, Rampton	4/85
SMU 726N	Daimler CRL6	MCW	H44/27D	1975	1/83	Young, Rampton	4/85
GHV 22N	Daimler CRL6	Park Royal	H44/27D	1975	5/83	London Transport (D1022)	4/85
THM 704M	Daimler CRL6	MCW	H45/32F	1974	5/83	London Transport (DM1704)	4/85
PAG 761H	Daimler CRG6	Alexander	H44/31F	1970	1/84	A1, Ardrossan	5/85

Note - MLK 556L, THM 712M and SMU 726N were new to London Transport (DMS556, DM1712 and DM1726)

THM 712M (left)
A vast number of ex-London DMS class were sold into an eager market, as they were the newest double-deckers available in quantity. Norfolk Bluebird operated five of the breed and a well-laden example arrives at Mildenhall RAF base in June 1984 for the annual Air Fete organised by USAF personnel.

G R Mills

SMU 726N (right)
Many of the DMS class were converted to single door by Ensign for a wide spectrum of customers. This example displays the original configuration at the Norfolk Showground Gala Day in September 1983. Ipswich AEC Regent III ADX 1 is at the rear with a pair of Clarke's, Swaffham, Volvo coaches in the background.

G R Mills

G W Osborne & Sons, 6 East Street, Tollesbury, Essex

Very much a family business, with the founder having 12 children, almost all of whom were involved with varying commitments in the early days of operations. Horse drawn transport was upgraded with motorisation in 1919 and a solid-tyred, open-top, open staircase double-deck ex National was tried in the 1920s but not replaced. A double-decker of much more advanced design was introduced during World War II, albeit basic by modern standards, to cope with the excess loadings during the restrictive years. From the introduction of this AEC engined utility there was consistently a double-decker with either a Southall built chassis or engine in the fleet for the next 35 years. In the true halcyon days of bus operation, ie the early post war years when passenger numbers were at an all time high, brand new double-deckers were justified. However it was the purchase of ex-London RTs and ex-AEC demonstrators for which the Osborne fleet became famous in the psv world. The double-deckers appeared on all the principal stage services which included two routes between Tollesbury and Colchester (one via Birch, the other via Layer-de-la-Haye); Tollesbury to Maldon; and Tollesbury to Witham via Tiptree and Kelvedon.

An impressive steel frame and brick infill garage was completed in 1965 at 62 New Road replacing a clutter of timber shelters that had been modified and extended from the earliest days of operations. The rolling stock continued to achieve some notoriety with the acquisition of a pair of ex SBG Bristol VRTs, which had escaped the mass transfer from SBG to NBC. These were joined by the pair of experimental Bristol VRL ex-demonstration buses. The intake of the five RTs in the late 50s and early 60s was equalled in the 80s by 5 ex-Dundee Fleetlines with Alexander bodies. After a series of prolonged negotiations, Hedingham Omnibuses acquired the business in February 1997, including the bulk of the fleet and the garage, although by this time the office had moved from 6 East Street to a portakabin on the garage forecourt. The take over included six double-deckers; two Fleetlines and the dual-door VR were promptly disposed of as only the single-door VR/ECWs found favour joining a large number of the same type in the Hedingham fleet.

Livery: duo red and white

Double-Deckers operated 1944 - 1997

	Reg	Chassis	Body	Seats	New	In	Ex	Out
	JVW 648	Daimler CWA6	Duple	L27/28R	1944	3/44	New	10/58
	UF 5538	Leyland TD1	Leyland	L24/24R	1930	4/46	Blackwell, Earls Colne	10/51
	MPU 530	Daimler CVD6	Strachan	L27/28R	1947	10/47	New	10/62
	PPU 982	AEC Regent III	Strachan	L27/28R	1950	2/50	New	6/66
	CCX 698	Daimler CWA6	Brush	L27/28R	1944	11/53	Benfleet Garages, Hadleigh	10/58
1	2046 F	AEC Regent V	Park Royal	L31/28RD	1957	5/57	New	2/73
2	HLX 222	AEC Regent III	Weymann	H30/26R	1947	2/58	London Transport (RT405)	9/67
4	HLW 191	AEC Regent III	Park Royal	H30/26R	1947	1/59	London Transport (RT204)	1/69
7	80 WMH	AEC Bridgemaster	Park Royal	H45/31R	1959	12/60	AEC demonstrator	5/76
11	2211 MK	AEC Bridgemaster	Park Royal	H43/29F	1960	6/61	AEC demonstrator	4/79
17	HLX 134	AEC Regent III	Park Royal	H30/26R	1948	5/63	London Transport (RT317)	9/68
18	8071 ML	AEC Renown	Park Royal	H44/31F	1962	11/63	AEC demonstrator	8/79
21	MXX 186	AEC Regent III	Weymann	H30/26R	1953	3/64	London Transport (RT3671)	4/71
39	LYR 997	AEC Regent III	Weymann	H30/26R	1952	6/65	London Transport (RT2827)	6/72
29	KXW 356	Leyland 6RT	Leyland	H30/26R	1950	7/66	London Transport (RTW256)	3/73
37	349 FTB	Guy Arab IV	NCME	H41/32R	1958	11/70	LUT (632)	9/75
6	YJG 808	AEC Bridgemaster	Park Royal	H43/29F	1962	6/72	East Kent	3/74
26	NAG 588G	Bristol VRT/SL6G	ECW	H43/32F	1969	1/73	Western SMT (2237)	12/84
27	OCS 581H	Bristol VRT/SL6G	ECW	H43/32F	1969	1/73	Western SMT (2251)	12/84
29	GGM 431D	Bristol VRLSL6G	ECW	H45/35F	1966	10/73	Bristol (C5000)	10/86
30	HHW 933D	Bristol VRLSL6G	ECW	H45/35F	1966	10/73	Bristol (C5001)	5/79
12	LLH 5K	Leyland PDR2/1	Roe	H45/24F	1972	3/75	Silverline, Hounslow	9/83
13	LLH 8K	Leyland PDR2/1	Roe	H45/24F	1972	3/75	Silverline, Hounslow	9/83
16	DAU 421C	Leyland PDR1/1	NCME	H44/33F	1965	9/77	Nottingham (421)	5/81
1	JKE 341E	Leyland PDR1/1	Massey	H43/31F	1967	12/77	Rapson, Brora	5/86
2	BVX 676B	Bristol FLF6B	ECW	H38/32F	1964	12/78	Eastern National (2800)	8/81
3	STW 764D	Bristol FLF6B	ECW	H38/32F	1966	8/79	Eastern National (2876)	8/83
4	SOE 967H	Daimler CRG6LX-33	Park Royal	H47/33D	1969	10/79	West Midlands (3967)	1/85
11	OSR 191R	Bristol VRT/LL3/6LXB	Alexander	H49/34D	1977	11/80	Tayside (191)	2/97
3	KUC 219P	Daimler CRL6	MCW	H45/32F	1975	5/83	London Transport (DMS1219)	12/87
2	KUC 228P	Daimler CRL6	MCW	H45/32F	1975	5/83	London Transport (DMS1228)	2/97
12	GSL 902N	Daimler CRG6LXB	Alexander	H49/34D	1975	3/84	Tayside (174)	7/95
18	GSL 901N	Daimler CRG6LXB	Alexander	H49/34D	1975	8/84	Tayside (173)	7/95
26	GSL 900N	Daimler CRG6LXB	Alexander	H49/34D	1975	11/84	Tayside (172)	11/92
27	GSL 899N	Daimler CRG6LXB	Alexander	H49/34D	1975	12/84	Tayside (171)	7/95
4	GSL 897N	Daimler CRG6LXB	Alexander	H49/38F	1975	2/85	Tayside (109)	2/97
15	EVY 696L	Daimler CRG6LX	Roe	H44/34F	1972	3/86	Prindale, Barwick-in-Elmet	9/90
3	OUC 38R	Leyland Fleetline	MCW	H44/33F	1977	1/88	Solent Blueline	8/94
12	CJH 115V	Bristol VRT/SL3/6LXB	ECW	H43/31F	1980	8/95	Stephensons, Hullbridge	2/97
27	CJH 141V	Bristol VRT/SL3/6LXB	ECW	H43/31F	1980	8/95	Stephensons, Hullbridge	2/97
18	BHJ 368S	Bristol VRT/SL3/6LXB	ECW	H43/31F	1980	9/95	Brentwood Coaches	2/97

The following vehicles were purchased but not operated:

Reg	Chassis	Body	Seats	New	In	Ex	Out
JXC26	AEC Regent III	Weymann	H30/26R	1948	10/63	London Transport (RT663)	4/66
HLX254	AEC Regent III	Park Royal	H30/26R	1947	3/67	Superb, Birmingham	2/68
KLB562	AEC Regent III	Park Royal	H30/26R	1950	3/67	Superb, Birmingham	2/68
DHD182	AEC Regent V	MCW	H39/31F	1958	1/71	Yorkshire Woollen	12/73

Notes:
UF 5538 was new to Southdown (838)
CCX 698 was new to Huddersfield (208)
HLX 254 was new to London Transport (RT437)
KLB 562 was new to London Transport (RT1313)
GGM 431D was new as a demonstrator with Western SMT (BN331)
HHW 933D was new as a demonstrator with Mansfield District (555)

JKE 341E was new to Maidstone (41)
EVY 696L was new to York Pullman (96)
OUC 38R was new to London Transport (DMS2038)
CJH 114/41V were new to Alder Valley (975, 601)
BHJ 368S was new to Alder Valley (952) and was previously registered HIL9273 until 8/95 and originally VPF282S until 10/93
LYR 997 and 8071 ML survived into preservation

(Ref: *Buses Annual 1977*, *Buses 507* June 1997, *Buses from Tollesbury* by Geoff Mills, published 1995 by MW Transport Publications)

MPU 530 (top left)

The first new double-decker to join the Osborne's fleet was a Daimler CVD6 with a Strachans body built in Acton, London. The stalwart survived for 15 years and is seen on a murky December day in 1961 in Goldhanger Road, Heybridge, returning home on service from Maldon.

G R Mills

PPU 982 (middle left)

The second new post-war double-decker for Osborne's fleet was also bodied by Strachans, but to a more curvaceous style. The bus survived for a full 16 years service with Osborne's and is seen climbing the Donkey & Buskins hill in Layer-de-la-Haye bound for Tollesbury with a full load during July 1962.

G R Mills

17: HLX 134 (bottom left)

Osborne's became very well known as operators of ex-London RT class buses from 1958 to 1972. The third example to join the fleet was former RT317 which fell foul of a low bridge at the appropriate Battlesbridge on the old Southend road. The bus is seen in Birch Street during April 1966, en route to Tollesbury fitted with the roof that had previously graced RTL72, an easy task thanks to LT standardisation.

G R Mills

1: 2046F (bottom right)

Always known as "Freddie" by the Osborne staff, the last new double-decker to enter the fleet was a stylish Park Royal bodied AEC Regent V, seen here in Colchester's Queen Street bus station in December 1967. After 16 years service from Tollesbury, the bus was painted blue by PVS (London) Ltd and put to work on the Lesney (Matchbox Toys) staff transport contract in Hackney before later export to the USA.

G R Mills

The front-engined era

80: 80 WMH (top right)
The second claim to fame began with the ex-demonstration AEC Bridgemaster which arrived at Tollesbury in a green livery. The bus, freshly repainted red, is seen leaving Colchester bus station in Queen Street, then newly opened, during July 1961, driven by the late Gilbert Osborne.

G R Mills

11: 2211 MK (top left)
The second Bridgemaster arrived in Birmingham City Transport livery of dark blue and cream with a sandpaper roof. Operated by Osborne's for 18 years, the bus is seen at rest beside the dovecote at the top of Queen Street bus station in April 1973.

G R Mills

29: KXW 356 (second from top right)
Very few of the 8ft wide ex-London RTW class found further service in the UK. Osborne's solitary example is seen returning home through Layer-de-la-Haye in July 1967 having worked a morning peak trip into Colchester. All the cream bands are carefully lined out in black.

G R Mills

18: 8071 ML (lower left)
The third AEC demonstrator to join the Osborne fleet was a Renown with an interesting pedigree, having worked for London Transport (Country Area) at Northfleet depot in Kent. From 1975 the front dome was replaced with one from a Bridgemaster, which was less curvaceous than the original, as seen at Malting Green, Layer-de-la-Haye, in April 1979.

G R Mills

6: YJG 808 (third from top right)
The last AEC double-decker to join the Osborne fleet was a second-hand Bridgemaster from East Kent, which retained the maroon and cream livery throughout its 2 year stay, as shown on the garage forecourt in July 1972.

G R Mills

3: STW 764D (lower right)
At a time when Osborne's front-engined double-deckers were being eliminated, a pair of Bristol-engined FLFs were acquired from Ensignbus, ex-Eastern National. These were promptly repainted into red and cream to avoid confusion with the previous owner's stock in Colchester, Maldon, Kelvedon and Witham and one is shown, newly outshopped, on the Tollesbury garage forecourt in September 1979.

G R Mills

26: NAG 588G (top left)

In the final three months of 1972, three ex-Western SMT Bristol VRTs went to S & N (dealers) of Bishopbriggs to test the independent operator market. Osborne's bought a pair but in the following year the Scottish Bus Group set up a scheme whereby all 91 remaining VRTs went south to National Bus Company in exchange for Bristol FLFs. One of the escapees is seen at Great Wigborough "Kings Head" in May 1983.

G R Mills

29: GGM 431D (top right and second from top right)

Osbornes achieved a further claim to fame in 1973 when they acquired the pair of Bristol VRL prototypes which had been exhibited at the 1966 Commercial Motor Show at Earls Court. From January 1967 to May 1970, GGM worked for Central SMT of Motherwell before returning home for service with Bristol Omnibus. With both operators, the bus had spent long periods out of service. By comparison, the bus was in semi-retirement at Tollesbury, normally working one journey to Colchester on weekdays and thus survived 16 years. Seen in Colchester bus station with red replacing the Bristol green in July 1974 and again in New Road, Tollesbury in June 1979 after a full repaint into Osborne's duo-red and white.

G R Mills

11: OSR 191R (lower right)

Attracted by a high capacity double-decker that was only three years old, Osborne's invested in one of the 25 Alexander bodied VRs which were new to Tayside (Dundee). Acquired via Ensignbus in a duo-blue livery, the bus was initially repainted dark red, eliminating the blue. The more attractive red and white livery applied at a subsequent repaint is clearly shown in this view at Tollesbury Square in October 1995.

G R Mills

27: CJH 141V (bottom left)

The last double-deckers bought by Osborne's were three very standard ECW bodied VRTs in 1995. One of these was used by the Omnibus Society for a tour of the main routes on the last day of operation by Osborne's prior to the Hedingham takeover; 27 is seen in Station Road, Tollesbury in February 1997.

G R Mills

13: LLH 8K (top left)
One of five Leyland Atlanteans specially built by Roe for a TWA contract at Heathrow Airport, hence a large luggage compartment at the rear of the lower deck. The vehicles were only three years old when sold and found ready buyers, including Limebourne; Smith of Buntingford and Cottrells, Mitcheldean. One of the Osborne pair is seen on Maldon Promenade during November 1977.

G R Mills

1: JKE 341E (second from top left)
The only Massey body to see service in the Osborne fleet was this ex-Maidstone example which was very similar to ten new to Colchester (numbers 45-54). Thus the latter met 1 whenever it was allocated to either of the two routes from Tollesbury into Colchester (via Birch or via Layer-de-la-Haye). On this occasion, 1 was working to Maldon when seen at Goldhanger in November 1979. Note the chalked sign advertising local produce for sale! The bus was later sold to Theobalds at Long Melford where it joined three other ex-Maidstone Massey bodied Atlanteans.

G R Mills

4: SOE 976H (top right)
The ex-WMPTE "Jumbos" were popular in Suffolk through Partridge & Son's success at the auctions in Birmingham and all three with Norfolk's of Nayland saw service into Colchester. On this occasion in November 1979, the Osborne example waits in Tollesbury Square before working a journey to Maldon. This bus was the first dual-door double-decker and the first Fleetline in Osborne's fleet, eight more Fleetlines were to follow.

G R Mills

3: OUC 38R (bottom right)
The third and final DMS to join the fleet, although Ensign had loaned a pair whilst Osborne's initial intake (2 and 3) were converted to single-door. Much travelled, the final example had seen service with the A1 group in Ardrossan and Solent Blueline in Southampton and even went to Fourways at Chelmsford after Osborne's. Seen here at Tollesbury Square in January 1988 freshly repainted.

G R Mills

12: GSL 902N (lower left)
The first of five Fleetlines that came south from Dundee, joining the VRT/Alexander from the same source. All were dual-door, except the final acquisition which was converted to single door by Ensignbus prior to purchase by Osborne's. 12 is seen on School Hill, Birch, on a very frosty Christmas Eve in 1992.

G R Mills

C J Partridge & Son Ltd, Mount Pleasant, George Street, Hadleigh, Suffolk

When the third generation took control of the business in 1956, the vehicle policy changed dramatically. Harry Claireaux, son-in-law, bought used rolling stock and, in 1961, introduced a double-decker into the fleet. Operations were centred on Portman's Farm in Lower Layham from 1916 until a large site was acquired in Hadleigh in 1964. The original premises were utilised for a large bungalow for the proprietor and his wife Dorothy (nee Partridge). Two services were operated into Ipswich and others into Bury St Edmunds and Stowmarket. There were also works services to BX Plastics at Brantham and CAV at Sudbury. Expansion first came in 1963 with the acquisition of Hitcham - Ipswich service of B A Taylor & Sons of Bildeston, although none of the all coach fleet was taken into stock. Secondly in October 1963, Cooksons of Lawford's contracts into BX Plastics were purchased together with a Bedford OB. The final gain were further contracts to BX Plastics from P & M of Ipswich, together with a double-decker, which was licensed to Harris (Progressive) of Cambridge until that company went into liquidation. Occasionally the ex-Eastern Counties PD1 was used on the busy ex-Taylor's route until the service was sold to PB Squirrell of Hitcham in March 1966.

The need for multiple double-deckers arose in 1977 when the contract for all the military personnel movements out of Eastern Command at Colchester was won. These were particularly required for such events as the annual tattoo when dozens of regiments were based at the camps and needed transfers to Castle Park where the show was held. Dealing, which had commenced from the larger Hadleigh site, reached an all time high in 1979 when a dozen Atlanteans were acquired direct from Lothian in Edinburgh, and concluded with nine VRs from Oxford. Other batches included Scottish Fleetlines, which came via Askins of Barnsley while the West Midland "Jumbo" Fleetlines came via BCA at Birmingham as the result of successful bids. In September 1994, twenty-four vehicles, including 3 DMSs, together with the contract and stage commitments passed to Hedingham Omnibuses Sudbury depot. Ironically, seven of the saloons returned to Hadleigh in a dealer capacity from 1995 to 1998.

After suffering a severe stroke, Harry died in May 1999. Two Fords (dealing stock), a double-deck coach and a saloon were cremated in a garage fire in October 1999 and this spelt the end of his daughter Gillian's aspirations of continuing the "Partridge Coaches" operation. The garage buildings were demolished and the site sold for housing.

Livery: originally red and cream; white, caramel and black from June 1972

Double-Deckers operated 1961 - 2000

Reg	Chassis	Body	Seats	New	In	Ex	Out
EX 5282	Guy Arab III	Park Royal	H30/26R	1944	9/61	Great Yarmouth (20)	8/62
JFJ 707	Daimler CVD6	Brush	H30/26R	1948	8/62	Exeter (44)	2/64
GPW 358	Leyland PD1A	ECW	L27/26R	1947	1/64	Eastern Counties (AP358)	10/66
DCK 213	Leyland PD2/3	East Lancs	FL27/26RD	1951	11/66	Bingley, Kinsley (Utd Services)	1/68
NEH 453	Leyland OPD2/1	NCME	L27/26RD	1949	11/68	Harris, Cambridge	4/69
JWY 225	Bristol KSW6B	ECW	L27/28RD	1950	3/69	West Yorkshire (DBW2)	3/71
VNO 859	Bristol KSW5G	ECW	L27/28RD	1952	11/70	Eastern National (2364)	11/71
OWX 167	Bristol LD6B	ECW	H33/27RD	1955	1/71	West Yorkshire (DX23)	12/71
THW 746	Bristol LD6B	ECW	H33/25RD	1955	12/71	Hedingham (L65)	8/76
399 COR	Dennis Loline III	Alexander	H39/29F	1961	7/76	Norfolk, Nayland	8/76
WFN 834	AEC Regent V	Park Royal	H40/32F	1961	3/77	East Kent	7/81
WFN 837	AEC Regent V	Park Royal	H40/32F	1961	3/77	East Kent	3/78
YJG 817	AEC Regent V	Park Royal	H40/32F	1962	4/77	East Kent	4/81
WFN 830	AEC Regent V	Park Royal	H40/32F	1961	3/78	East Kent	4/81
WFN 840	AEC Regent V	Park Royal	H40/32F	1961	3/78	East Kent	4/81
SOE 956H	Daimler CRG6LX	Park Royal	H47/33D	1969	9/79	West Midlands PTE (3956)	11/79
SOE 941H	Daimler CRG6LX	Park Royal	H47/33D	1969	11/79	West Midlands PTE (3941)	9/80
JSC 857E	Leyland PDR1/1	Alexander	H43/31F	1967	5/80	Lothian (857)	11/82
JSC 886E	Leyland PDR1/1	Alexander	H43/31F	1967	6/80	Lothian (886)	1/83
JSC 859E	Leyland PDR1/1	Alexander	H43/31F	1967	8/80	Lothian (859)	8/83
JSC 890E	Leyland PDR1/1	Alexander	H43/31F	1967	9/80	Lothian (890)	9/82
SOE 978H	Daimler CRG6LX	Park Royal	H47/33D	1969	5/81	West Midlands PTE (3978)	9/82
SOE 970H	Daimler CRG6LX	Park Royal	H47/33D	1969	6/81	West Midlands PTE (3970)	4/82
SOE 971H	Daimler CRG6LX	Park Royal	H47/33D	1969	5/82	West Midlands PTE (3971)	9/82
TOB 997H	Daimler CRG6LX	Park Royal	H47/33D	1969	5/82	West Midlands PTE (3997)	11/91
SOE 975H	Daimler CRG6LX	Park Royal	H47/33D	1969	9/82	West Midlands PTE (3975)	7/92
PRG 132J	Daimler CRG6LX	Alexander	H48/32D	1971	9/82	Grampian (132)	9/84
PRG 134J	Daimler CRG6LX	Alexander	H48/32D	1971	9/82	Grampian (134)	12/84
PRG 135J	Daimler CRG6LX	Alexander	H48/32D	1971	9/82	Grampian (135)	1/88
PRG 137J	Daimler CRG6LX	Alexander	H48/32D	1971	9/82	Grampian (137)	12/82
PRG 138J	Daimler CRG6LX	Alexander	H48/32D	1971	2/83	Dunmoy, Rochdale	4/83
PYJ 464L	Daimler CRG6LXB	Alexander	H49/34D	1973	2/83	Tayside (464)	9/83

Reg	Chassis	Body	Seats	New	In	Ex	Out
HUA 556N	Scania BR111DH	MCW	H45/30F	1975	4/83	West Yorkshire PTE (2605)	9/84
PYJ 458L	Daimler CRG6LXB	Alexander	H49/34D	1973	9/83	Tayside (458)	4/85
PRG 131J	Daimler CRG6LX	Alexander	H48/32D	1971	6/84	Moffat & Williamson, Gauldry	8/84
PYJ 459L	Daimler CRG6LXB	Alexander	H49/34D	1973	8/84	Tayside (459)	9/84
PYJ 460L	Daimler CRG6LXB	Alexander	H49/34D	1973	8/84	Tayside (460)	7/92
PRG 141J	Daimler CRG6LX	Alexander	H48/32D	1971	9/85	Moffat & Williamson, Gauldry	7/92
THM 630M	Daimler CRL6	MCW	H44/33F	1974	12/85	Morris (CK), Cardiff	9/94
THM 647M	Daimler CRL6	MCW	H44/33F	1974	12/85	Morris (CK), Cardiff	10/94
GHM 825N	Daimler CRL6	MCW	H44/29D	1975	3/87	Coach Services, Thetford	7/92
GGG 306N	Leyland AN68/1R	Alexander	H45/31F	1975	9/87	Coach Services, Thetford	7/92
KUC 989P	Leyland Fleetline	MCW	H45/32F	1976	4/88	Premier Travel (314)	10/92
KJD 58P	Leyland Fleetline	Park Royal	H45/32F	1976	7/88	Premier Travel (311)	8/93
KJD 24P	Leyland Fleetline	MCW	H45/32F	1976	8/88	Premier Travel (310)	10/91
OJD 126R	Leyland Fleetline	Park Royal	H45/34F	1976	8/88	Ementon, Cranfield	9/94
JGA 206N	Leyland AN68/1R	Alexander	H45/31F	1975	9/88	London Country NE (AN323)	8/89
DAU 379C	AEC Renown	Weymann	O40/30F	1965	10/91	Hedingham (L179)	6/96
GNS 672N	Leyland AN68/1R	Alexander	H45/31F	1975	11/91	Fowler, Holbeach Drove	7/92
HHB 48N	Leyland AN68/1R	East Lancs	H44/32F	1974	6/92	Waddon, Caerphilly	10/94
GGM 76W	Bristol VRT/SL3/6LXB	ECW	H43/31F	1981	9/92	City of Oxford (1534)	10/92
GGM 109W	Bristol VRT/SL3/6LXB	ECW	H43/31F	1981	9/92	City of Oxford (1542)	10/92
HJB 460W	Bristol VRT/SL3/6LXB	ECW	H43/31F	1980	9/92	City of Oxford (1553)	10/92
HJB 463W	Bristol VRT/SL3/6LXB	ECW	H43/31F	1980	9/92	City of Oxford (1556)	10/92
AUD 463R	Bristol VRTSL3/6LXB	ECW	H43/31F	1976	10/92	Maybury, Cranborne	4/94
THX 324S	Leyland Fleetline	MCW	H45/23D	1978	11/92	London Buses (DMS2324)	9/94
SWW 300R	Bristol VRT/SL3/6LXB	ECW	H43/31F	1977	4/93	Capital Citybus	4/94
VOD 592S	Bristol VRT/SL3/6LXB	ECW	H43/31F	1978	4/93	Capital Citybus (502)	4/94
RLG 428V	Bristol VRT/SL3/501	ECW	H43/31F	1980	4/94	Cavern City, Liverpool	9/96
BFR 301R	Leyland AN68A/1R	East Lancs	H50/36F	1977	8/94	Cedric, Wivenhoe	9/94
BFR 302R	Leyland AN68A/1R	East Lancs	H50/36F	1977	8/94	Sheffield Omnibus	3/95
SGR 791V	Bristol VRT/SL3/6LXB	ECW	H43/31F	1980	8/97	Wright, Newark	5/00

Vehicles owned but not operated:

Reg	Chassis	Body	Seats	New	In	Ex	Out
WFN 833	AEC Regent V	Park Royal	H40/32F	1961	3/77	East Kent	9/78
NCK 372	Leyland PDR1/1	Metro-Cammell	H44/34F	1959	1/79	Harwich & Dovercourt (2)	8/79
NCK 630	Leyland PDR1/1	Metro-Cammell	H44/34F	1959	3/79	Royal Navy (46RN42)	8/79
NRN 584	Leyland PDR1/1	Metro-Cammell	H44/34F	1960	3/79	Royal Navy (46RN43)	4/81
JSC 858E	Leyland PDR1/1	Alexander	H43/31F	1967	12/79	Lothian (858)	8/83
JSC 865E	Leyland PDR1/1	Alexander	H43/31F	1967	12/79	Lothian (865)	5/81
JSC 883E	Leyland PDR1/1	Alexander	H43/31F	1967	12/79	Lothian (883)	4/80
JSC 888E	Leyland PDR1/1	Alexander	H43/31F	1967	12/79	Lothian (888)	6/83
JSC 889E	Leyland PDR1/1	Alexander	H43/31F	1967	12/79	Lothian (889)	8/83
JSC 892E	Leyland PDR1/1	Alexander	H43/31F	1967	12/79	Lothian (892)	8/90
JSC 893E	Leyland PDR1/1	Alexander	H43/31F	1967	12/79	Lothian (893)	4/80
JSC 894E	Leyland PDR1/1	Alexander	H43/31F	1967	12/79	Lothian (894)	9/81
6198KW	AEC Regent V	Metro-Cammell	H40/30F	1963	3/80	Carter, Litcham	4/80
BON 496C	Daimler CRG6LX	Park Royal	H44/33F	1965	3/81	West Midlands PTE (3496)	6/81
FOC 604D	Daimler CRG6LX	Metro-Cammell	H43/33F	1966	3/81	West Midlands PTE (3604)	6/81
SOE 906H	Daimler CRG6LX	Park Royal	H47/33D	1969	5/81	West Midlands PTE (3906)	4/82
SOE 927H	Daimler CRG6LX	Park Royal	H47/33D	1969	5/81	West Midlands PTE (3927)	5/83
HPV 34	AEC Regent V	Park Royal	H37/28R	1959	4/82	Townsend Thoresen, Felixstowe	5/84
SOE 923H	Daimler CRG6LX	Park Royal	H47/33D	1969	12/82	Young, Rampton	5/83
SOE 934H	Daimler CRG6LX	Park Royal	H47/33D	1969	12/82	Young, Rampton	5/83
SOE 953H	Daimler CRG6LX	Park Royal	H47/33D	1969	12/82	Clarke, Swaffham	5/83
HUA 565N	Scania BR111DH	MCW	H45/30F	1975	8/84	West Yorkshire PTE (2614)	8/88
HUA 587N	Scania BR111DH	MCW	H45/30F	1975	8/84	West Yorkshire PTE (2636)	8/88
RYG 664R	Scania BR111DH	MCW	H43/31F	1977	8/84	West Yorkshire PTE (2664)	4/85
TGX 821M	Daimler CRL6	Park Royal	H44/27D	1974	2/86	Wealden, Feltham	8/88
TGX 855M	Daimler CRL6	Park Royal	H--D	1974	3/86	Artists International, London W1	7/88
ABN 201B	Leyland PDR1/1	East Lancs	H45/33F	1964	1/88	Theobald, Long Melford	2/88
GHJ 381L	Daimler CRL6-33	NCME	H49/31D	1973	7/89	Rannoch, Haughley (X)	8/89
JKE 337E	Leyland PDR1/1	Massey	H43/31F	1967	8/89	Theobald, Long Melford	8/89
PRG 126J	Daimler CRG6LX	Alexander	H48/35F	1971	3/91	Norfolk, Nayland	10/94
JUS 778N	Leyland AN68/1R	Alexander	H45/31F	1975	11/91	Fowler, Holbeach Drove	4/92
THM 678M	Daimler CRL6	MCW	H--F	1974	10/92	Fenland Resource Unit, Wisbech (X)	3/93
SOE 956H	Daimler CRG6LX	Park Royal	H--D	1969	12/92	Gardiner, Finningham (X)	3/93
TMA 331R	Bristol VRT/SL3/501	ECW	H43/31F	1976	3/93	City Fleet, Bootle (103)	10/94
WPV 88L	Leyland AN68/1R	Roe	H43/29D	1973	9/94	Glaxo, Stevenage	10/94
URN 152R	Bristol VRT/SL3/6LXB	East Lancs	H43/32F	1976	9/94	Hunter, Garston (V16)	10/94
WTG 357T	Bristol VRT/SL3/6LXB	Alexander	H43/31F	1978	11/94	Cardiff (357)	5/00
SNJ 592R	Bristol VRT/SL3/6LXB	ECW	H43/31F	1977	10/96	Oxford (443)	11/96
AAP 651T	Bristol VRT/SL3/6LXB	ECW	H43/31F	1978	10/96	Oxford (444)	9/97
EAP 989V	Bristol VRT/SL3/6LXB	ECW	H43/31F	1980	10/96	Oxford (446)	11/96
EAP 999V	Bristol VRT/SL3/6LXB	ECW	H43/31F	1980	10/96	Oxford (447)	10/96
HJB 451W	Bristol VRT/SL3/6LXB	ECW	H43/31F	1980	10/96	Oxford (451)	2/97
HJB 452W	Bristol VRT/SL3/6LXB	ECW	H43/31F	1980	10/96	Oxford (452)	2/97
HJB 454W	Bristol VRT/SL3/6LXB	ECW	H43/31F	1980	10/96	Oxford (454)	2/97
HJB 457W	Bristol VRT/SL3/6LXB	ECW	H43/31F	1980	10/96	Oxford (457)	7/99

Reg	Chassis	Body	Seats	New	In	Ex	Out
HJB 461W	Bristol VRT/SL3/6LXB	ECW	H43/31F	1980	10/96	Oxford (461)	9/97
UAS 65T	Leyland Fleetline	ECW	H43/32F	1979	12/97	Highland Country (D321)	7/99
UAS 63T	Leyland Fleetline	ECW	H43/32F	1979	12/97	Highland Country (D319)	4/98
HTC 729N	Bristol VRT/SL2/6G	ECW	H39/31F	1975	1/98	Lapage, North Shoebury	7/98

Notes:

DCK 213 was new to Ribble (1242)
NEH 453 was new to PMT (L453) and originally had a Weymann B35F body
THW 746 was new to Bristol (L8256)
399 COR was new to Aldershot & District (399)
PRG 131/8/41J were new to Aberdeen (later Grampian) (131/8/41)
THM 630/47M, GHM825N were new to London Transport (DMS1630/47, 1825)
GGG306N was later registered 129SDV in 1/90 and KBJ 396N in 7/92, and was new to Glasgow (LA854)
KUC 989P, KJD 24, 58P were new to London Transport (DMS1989, 2024/58)
JGA 206N was new to Glasgow (LA927)
DAU 379C was new to Nottingham (379)
GNS 672N was new to Glasgow (LA880)
HHB 48N was new to Rhymney Valley (21)
GGM 76, 109W were new to Alder Valley (606/29)
HJB 460/3W were new to Alder Valley (640/3)
AUD 463R was new to Oxford (463)
SWW 300R was new to West Yorkshire (3975)
VOD 592S was new to Western National (582)

RLG 428V was new to Crosville (DVL428)
BFR 301/2R were new to Blackpool (301/2)
SGR 791V was new to United (791)

NCK 372, NCK 630, NRN 584 were new to Ribble (1631/41/84)
HPV 34 was new to Ipswich (34)
SOE 923/34/53H were new to West Midlands PTE (3923/34/53)
TGX 821/55M were new to London Transport (DMS821/55)
ABN 201B was new to Bolton (201), later SELNEC (6701)
GHJ 381L was new to Southend (381)
JKE 337E was new to Maidstone (37)
PRG 126J was new to Aberdeen (later Grampian) (126)
JUS 778N was new to Glasgow (LA931)
THM 678M was new to London Transport (DMS1678)
SOE 956H was new to West Midlands PTE (3956)
TMA 331R was new to Crosville (DVL331)
WPV 88L was new to Ipswich (88)
URN 152R was new to Burnley & Pendle (152)
SNJ 592R, AAP 651T, EAP 989/99V were new to Southdown (592, 651/89/99)
HJB 451/2/4/7/61W were new to Alder Valley (631/2/4/7/41)
HTC 729N was new to Bristol (5502)

VNO 859 and TOB 997H have both survived into preservation
(Ref: *Buses Extra 22*, 1982, and *Classic Bus 71*, June/July 2004)

GPW 358 (right)

Originally one of 20 Leyland PD1s with ECW bodies supplied to Eastern Counties in 1947, a fleet that normally only had new Bristol double-deckers in the post war years under Tilling, BTC and National Bus ownership. Four others of the batch came to East Anglian psv operators and 358 was the first Partridge double-decker to gain the red and cream livery as shown in this May 1964 shot at the Portman's Farm depot in Lower Layham. The author and photographer passed his psv test on the "beast" the following year.

G R Mills

DCK 213 (right)

With the unmistakeable styling of an ex-Ribble Leyland PD2/East Lancs, this was one of 20 supplied in 1950/1 as the second batch of the famed "White Lady" class. Despite demotion to stage carriage duties in February 1961, the dual-purpose type seating was retained through to withdrawal. Eleven of the batch were operated by the equally well known Premier Travel of Cambridge but 213 is seen here on 1 January 1967 at Hintlesham, Suffolk.

G R Mills

℗ARTRIDGE & SON

OWX 167 and JWY 225 (right)
Lined up on the last day in service for JWY 225, this 1950 Bristol KSW6B is seen with its replacement, OWX 167, a 1955 Bristol LD6B. Both vehicles were new to West Yorkshire Road Car and both had platform doors. Both buses were sampled by members of The PSV Circle (Colchester meeting) hence this posed shot at Hadleigh Swimming Pool car park in March 1971.

G R Mills

YJG 817, WFN 830, WFN 834 and WFN 840 (left)
Four of the five ex-East Kent AEC Regent Vs operated by Partridges are seen in Hyderabad Barracks, Colchester, during Tattoo week in August 1978. Each bus is labelled for the regimental bands which were conveyed to the Castle Park in Colchester where the event was held.

G R Mills

SOE 978H (bottom right)
The later paint style utilised less black and caramel and added more white producing a more modern appearance. This bus later passed to Norfolk's of Nayland but is seen in Hadleigh during June 1981.

G R Mills

JSC 886E (right)
Partridges purchased twelve from a batch of 50 originally supplied to Edinburgh in December 1979. Four were prepared for service and used and four were sold direct to other East Anglian psv operators. 886 is seen in March 1980 with Partridge vinyls on the original owners smart madder and white livery. This bus later passed to Ford, Althorne, Essex, who acquired four of the dozen.

G R Mills

SOE 956H (bottom left)
The first of six ex West Midlands PTE Fleetline "Jumbos" displays the livery style applied to the first pair and is seen in September 1979 in East Bergholt. The bus was later sold to Goldsmiths but returned to Partridges via a non psv owner 13 years later.

G R Mills

ARTRIDGE & SON

HUA 556N

Introduced in the UK in 1973, the Metropolitan used a Scania designed structure built in Britain by MCW. Four of the 95 supplied to West Yorkshire PTE were acquired by Partridges but only one, illustrated top right, was operated. Never popular with the fitters, the bus was sold to Emblings of Guyhirn, Cambridgeshire, for further service and is seen here when freshly repainted in April 1983.

G R Mills

THM 630M (second from top)

Of the many ex-London DMS class buses that had been initially converted to single door by Ensignbus that became available on the "third-hand" market, Partridges gained seven. The first such was an ex-CK of Cardiff example which had a row of vertical moulding lines in the area of the former centre door that were not fitted by Ensign! Seen on service in the Old Cattle Market bus station in Ipswich in September 1988.

G R Mills

GGG 306N (129 SDV/KBJ 896N) (third from top)

Taken in part exchange against a Bedford YRT/Plaxton coach, this 12-year old Leyland Atlantean received the cherished registration mark 129 SDV in January 1980, followed by a full repaint in October 1980, as seen at the yard when freshly completed. The bus was sold as KBJ 896N, the special mark being transferred to a Leyland Tiger/Duple Laser.

G R Mills

HHB 48N (bottom right)

This was one of a pair new in March 1975 to Rhymney Valley (formed in 1974 by the amalgamation of Caerphilly UDC, Gelligaer UDC and Bedwas & Machen UDC). The origins of the livery are obviously Stagecoach, utilised by the previous owner and over painted by Partridges as seen in May 1992.

G R Mills

AUD 463R (bottom left)

Originally supplied to City of Oxford in poppy red, later being transferred to South Midland and repainted maroon and cream, in 1987 this VR gained the special "Orbiter" striped livery. By the time this shot was taken in February 1993, the bus was in mundane white, as was the one time South Wales Neoplan/Plaxton 4000 (C357 KEP) in the Hadleigh garage. Both vehicles came from Maybury of Cranborne.

G R Mills

Colin S Pegg, Colberville, Caston, Norfolk

Colin had been employed as a PSV driver by Norman J Peeke-Vout prior to the purchase of his employers business in April 1953, together with three diminutive Bedfords. The first heavyweight coach, a Maudslay Marathon III, had a lasting influence on the fleet. Acquired from Robinson's of Great Harwood, the mid green and black livery was adopted for subsequent vehicles for the next 15 years.

The sixties saw considerable expansion, initially with the takeover of the services and one vehicle (an Albion/Duple) of D Goff of Hingham. Goff had acquired these from haulage contractor Rix of Foulsham in September 1958. Several heavyweight coaches were added to the fleet strength, the most startling of which was a Leyland Royal Tiger with Mann Egerton ½ decker (interlaced seating) bodywork which was operated for 4 years before being sold into preservation. By the time the W Carter of Marham business was added to Pegg's output, in April 1964, the feet had swayed towards a Bedford/Duple bias and the pair from Carter's fitted in well. In the same year the Swaffham premises and workings of A F Braybrooke were acquired, although no vehicles changed hands.

The importance of RAF Marham led to the purchase of an AEC Reliance/Willowbrook bus seating 65 in 1965, however the following year double-deckers were introduced to cope with school contracts. The need for high capacity coaches brought the Bedford VAL into the fleet, one such example, ex-Little, Annan, received such favourable comments from the Norfolk folk that Colin adopted the dual pink livery as his own. In June 1964, a pair of used Bedford coaches were acquired for the rail replacement service from Watton to Thetford. Ten years later the service still prospered although the commuters had diminished but the transport of scholars to Thetford Grammar school had increased such that, with British Rail assistance and generous new bus grants the acquisition of a NEW double-decker was justified. Apart from the National bus company Eastern Counties and Great Yarmouth municipal undertaking, new double-deckers, particularly with an independent operator, were rare in Norfolk. Adorned in the duo-pink, the bus was built as part of a batch for Leeds at a cost of £17,000 and became something of a sensation in the East Anglian operating world.

From 1980 the fleet was reduced, by then all the services which operated every weekday had been withdrawn leaving only market day and Saturday workings. The Swaffham property was sold to Payne Brothers of Norfolk Tyres and was subsequently occupied by ATS. The original Caston premises were still in use when three Bedford/Plaxton coaches and the surviving services passed to Jack Bridges (t/a Eniway Coaches) of Saham Toney in February 1995.

Livery: Initially green and black, duo pink from 1971

Double-Deckers operated 1966 - 1980

Reg	Chassis	Body	Seats	New	In	Ex	Out
EX 6561	Leyland PD2/1	Leyland	H30/26R	1949	10/66	Great Yarmouth 61	7/69
EX 6569	Leyland PD2/1	Leyland	H30/26R	1949	10/66	Great Yarmouth 69	8/67
KGK 786	Leyland 7RT	Weymann	H30/26RD	1949	3/68	London Transport (RTL122)	7/74
HCT 150	AEC Regent III	Strachan	H32/28RD	1953	12/67	Delaine, Bourne (39)	6/71
MWY 116	Bristol LD6B	ECW	H33/25RD	1953	3/71	West Yorkshire (DX7)	8/74
6989 AD	AEC Regent V	Willowbrook	H37/26F	1960	9/72	Delaine, Bourne (63)	9/75
SPW 92N	Leyland AN68/2R	Roe	H45/33D	1974	9/74	New	9/80

Notes:
6989 AD was new to Cotterell, Mitcheldean   SPW 92N was originally intended to be registered RVF 564M
HCT 150 was not licenced to operate for Pegg until 7/69

6989 AD

This exceptional AEC Regent V was eagerly purchased from the well-respected Delaine fleet where it had been the only example of the model. In fact the only other AEC double-decker owned by Delaine had also been purchased by Colin Pegg seven years earlier. The Delaine additions to the bodywork can easily be seen in this July 1973 view at Pegg's Caston premises - swoops to the upper and lower deck bands and around the destination box which boldly shows its previous home on the blind!

G R Mills

E E Pilbeam (t/a Harwich & Dovercourt Coaches), Nelson Road, Dovercourt, Essex
Chartercoach (Harwich) Ltd, High Street, Great Oakley, Essex

From a humble start in April 1962 with an 11-seat Ford/Martin Walter, the company progressed through a variety of Bedford models until early 1973 when an ex-Grey-Green Leyland Leopard/Harrington and a double-decker were taken into stock. The principal task for the latter was the transfer of Prins Ferries passengers from Harwich Rail Station to the Navyard Wharf. So popular was the Loline with the Germans from Bremerhaven and Hamburg that it was purchased by an admiring passenger and exported to Frassenden. Two more similar models were promptly acquired and repainted in a striking red and grey livery sporting illuminated offside adverts for Prins Ferries with the slogan "Sail Away Direct to Germany". A third double-decker joined the Lolines the same year and received the same livery with the addition of the UK and German national flag colours in bands on the between deck panels together with the shipping line's logos. With the registration NCK, the bus was referred to as Nick, which was confusing as the proprietor's son was also called Nick; he was at the helm following his father's death in August 1976.

A limited company was formed in July 1978 and over the next two years a pair of new Bedford coaches were purchased for tour work, much of which never materialised. Around this time severe structural problems with the house and workshop proved to be an impossible burden on the stability of the enterprise. In 1981, Derek Betts, one time manager of Harwich & Dovercourt, and later at Staines Crusader Holidays, Clacton-on-Sea, gained a controlling interest in the company. Double-deck operation was reintroduced after nearly three years absence together with large capacity saloons for school contracts. For the 1983 holiday season, an ex-London DMS was painted in Butlin's house colours of blue and yellow to provide a licensed stage service from Clacton Rail Station to the holiday camp at the Jaywick end of the seafront.

In the same year other major developments had taken place within the company. The long established business of R W Hooks Ltd, with operations dating back to 1919 was merged with Harwich & Dovercourt in March whilst in October CharterCoach (Harwich) Ltd was formed. None of the Hooks fleet, which was owned by Staines Crusader of Clacton, passed to the new occupiers of the Great Oakley premises, which remained in Hooks family ownership. By July 1986, any vehicles that remained licensed to Harwich & Dovercourt had been disposed of so that the entire fleet based in High Street Great Oakley was operated on CharterCoach licences.

On 1 September 1986 CharterCoach launched into the service bus market using six Leyland Leopards with Willowbrook C51F bodies in an unrelieved bright red livery with Coastal Red fleetnames on a service from Harwich via Great Oakley and Manningtree to Colchester in direct competition with Eastern National. One of the Leopards was later reseated with 53 bus seats. Expansion into Clacton followed on 26 January 1987, linking the town with Harwich and providing local bus services within the seaside resort for which a clutch ex-West Midlands PTE Fleetlines were acquired. Coastal Red was also successful with tenders for 16 Essex County Council contracted services for which an increased fleet was required. This brought objections from Great Oakley residents so a new operating centre was secured in Clacton at Telford Road on the Gorse Lane Industrial Estate. Formerly a Fiat commercial vehicle centre, the premises were renamed Charter House by CharterCoach in June 1987 and renamed again to Coastline House when Eastern National acquired the Coastal red operations and vehicles on 28 February 1988.

Chartercoach returned to Great Oakley but moved to Refinery Road, Parkeston Quay in 1992 only to be acquired by Abridge Enterprises (Supreme Coaches) of Hadleigh, Essex in January 1994. The Great Oakley garage was demolished and a new bungalow was built for Pru Hooks the daughter of R W Hooks.

Livery: duo green (Hooks)
red and grey (Harwich & Dovercourt)
orange & black(CharterCoach)
red (Coastal Red)

1, 2, 3: RDB 868, NCK 372 and RDB 889
Pilbeams on parade at Dovercourt Rail Station in November 1975 where the two ex-North Western Lolines flank the then newly acquired Leyland Atlantean. All were prepared to high standard by Nick Pilbeam; note the wheel trims. The slogan on the Atlantean was added long before the days of texting!

G R Mills

Double-Deckers operated 1953 - 1988

	Reg	Chassis	Body	Seats	New	In	Ex	Out
Hooks (owned but not operated):								
	CXX 324	AEC Regent	LPTB	H30/26R	1936	12/53	London Transport (STL1613)	5/55
Harwich & Dovercourt								
2	410COR	Dennis Loline III	Alexander	H39/29F	1961	5/73	Ipswich Coach Co (18)	10/75
1	RDB878	Dennis Loline III	Alexander	H39/32F	1960	7/75	SELNEC (878)	12/76
3	RDB889	Dennis Loline III	Alexander	H39/32F	1960	10/75	SELNEC (889)	9/77
2	NCK372	Leyland PDR1/1	Metro-Cammell	H44/34F	1959	11/75	Ribble (1631)	1/79
	SOE922H	Daimler CRG6LX	Park Royal	H47/33D	1970	9/81	Hornsby, Ashby	9/83
	KUC245P	Daimler CRL6	MCW	H44/27D	1975	11/81	Boon, Boreham	12/81
	SMU721N	Daimler CRL6	MCW	H44/24D	1975	11/82	London Transport (DM1721)	1/83
	THM518M	Daimler CRL6	MCW	H44/24D	1974	1/83	London Transport (DMS1518)	2/83
	JGF392K	Daimler CRG6	Park Royal	H45/28D	1972	4/83	London Transport (DMS392)	1/84
	THM719M	Daimler CRL6	MCW	H44/27D	1974	9/83	London Transport (DM1719)	1/84
	THM707M	Daimler CRL6	MCW	H44/27D	1974	12/83	London Transport (DM1707)	1/84
Harwich & Dovercourt (owned but not operated):								
	BCS984C	Daimler CRG6	Alexander	H44/31F	1965	3/83	Kelvedon Coaches	9/83
	DAU 432C	Leyland PDR1/2	Metro-Cammell	O44/33F	1965	3/83	Kelvedon Coaches	2/84
Chartercoach								
	EOF275L	Daimler CRG6LX	Park Royal	H43/33F	1973	11/86	West Midlands Travel (4275)	2/88
	EOF276L	Daimler CRG6LX	Park Royal	H43/33F	1973	11/86	West Midlands Travel (4276)	12/86
	GOG558N	Daimler CRG6LX	Park Royal	H43/33F	1973	12/86	West Midlands Travel (4558)	2/88
	NOB331M	Daimler CRG6LX	Park Royal	H43/33F	1975	12/86	West Midlands Travel (4331)	2/88
	EOF246L	Daimler CRG6LX	Park Royal	H43/33F	1973	1/87	West Midlands Travel (4246)	2/88
	JOV700P	Bristol VRTSL2/6LX	MCW	H43/33F	1975	7/87	West Midlands Travel (4700)	2/88
	JOV703P	Bristol VRTSL2/6LX	MCW	H43/33F	1975	7/87	West Midlands Travel (4703)	2/88
	JOV720P	Bristol VRTSL2/6LX	MCW	H43/33F	1975	7/87	West Midlands Travel (4720)	2/88
	GOG632N	Bristol VRTSL2/6LX	MCW	H43/33F	1974	9/87	West Midlands Travel (4632)	2/88

Notes:
410 COR was new to Aldershot & District (410)
SOE 922H was new to West Midlands PTE (3922)
KUC 245P was new to London transport (DM2245)
THM 518M, SMU 721N and KUC 245P were on short term loan
from Ensign, Purfleet.

BCS 984C was new to Western SMT (R2001)
EOF 246/75/6L, NOB 331M, GOG 558N, GOG 632N, JOV
700/3/20P were new to West Midlands PTE (4246/75/6, 4331,
4558, 4632, 4700/3/20)

(Ref: *Buses 398* May 1988 and *Essex Bus Enthusiasts Group Fact File 4*, published 2003)

JOV 703P
The scene in Colchester and Clacton was much
enlivened throughout 1987 by the daily appearances of
the Coast Red fleet operating in direct competition with
Eastern National. One of the rare Bristol VRT/MCW is
seen departing Colchester bus station in January 1988
on service 174 to Clacton via Wivenhoe, Alresford and St
Osyth. The bus was withdrawn the following month and
the 174 was replaced by Eastern National commercial
service 74.

G R Mills

GOG 558N
With the advance into Clacton, a further 4 ex-West
Midlands double-deckers were acquired (as illustrated
above). One of the original batch of five Daimler
Fleetlines was route branded for the hourly Clacton
Circular 50/50A. Initially displaying a large "30p Flat
Fare" sign, this had been removed by the time this view
in Station Road, Clacton-on-Sea, was taken in February
1988, a fortnight before the facility ceased.

G R Mills

Chartercoach DMS Delights

JGF 392K (top right)
Chartercoach consistently bought new Berkhof bodied coaches from 1983-1986, amassing six supplied by Ensignbus during that period. Thus it was no surprise that six ex-London DMS class double-deckers would be sourced from the same dealer. The oldest, and only Gardner powered example, is seen on Hythe Quay, Colchester, in April 1983 as an all-over advert for Butlins at Clacton in the holiday camp's house colours of blue and yellow.

G R Mills

JGF 392K (top left)
After Butlins closed the Clacton holiday camp, another enterprise took over the site and named it Atlas Park. Accordingly the former Butlins livery disappeared in favour of eye-catching bold lettering and cartoon-style impressions of the various attractions on the site. The bus is seen at Great Oakley garage about to set out for Clacton Rail station in September 1984. THM 707M was in an identical livery in the same period.

G R Mills

THM 719M (lower right)
The standard Chartercoach livery applied to both THM 707M and 719M was orange and black as displayed on 719 arriving in Colchester Bus Station in September 1983 having discharged DFDS shipping line passengers in Cowdray Crescent (Castle Park Gates/War Memorial), an operation that frequently required all three DMSs then operated. The work passed to Supreme Travel of Hadleigh, Essex, when Chartercoach ceased trading.

G R Mills

THM 719M (lower left)
The daily day trips to France organised by Adrian Loveridge, t/a Incentive Travel of West Mersea were very popular in the 1980s when day passports were available. 719 was tastefully repainted in cream and coffee as an all-over advert for the trips which were operated by from 1982 to 1986 by Berkhof bodied coaches in the same livery, the double-decker staying in the UK! 719 is seen freshly outshopped at Great Oakley in August 1984. Incentive Travel bought two pairs of Setra coaches in their own name, based at Marks Tey, but ceased operations in 1989.

G R Mills

A Towler & Sons Ltd, 65 London Road, Brandon, Suffolk

Towler's was established by the late-thirties, with a wide variety of used makes and models including Crossley, Dennis and REO chassis, as well as Gilford AS6, 166SD and Hera. The latter was ex Alexander of Falkirk, as was a Leyland Cheetah/Burlingham which was operated for 20 years. The early post-war years saw new Bedford OB and SB models taken into stock (3 of each) and four used Bedford OBs which eradicated the "odd-balls" and presented a standardised, modern fleet.

In the fifties, Towler's provided market day services to Bury St Edmunds, Kings Lynn, Ely and Downham Market. These were well loaded and frequently required relief vehicles, which ultimately led to the decision to operate double-deck buses. An important trio of licensed stage services were operated in the sixties and seventies for the Mills, Cartwright & Reynolds clothing manufacturers workforce in Millers Lane, Brandon. The factory was later occupied by MultiYork, furniture manufacturers, and was later developed for housing. The coaches were always well presented and regularly sourced from well-known fleets including Wallace Arnold, Samuel Ledgard (4) and Ulsterbus (3). The latter trio were the first examples of Northern Ireland-registered coaches operating in East Anglia.

During 1974, F G Carter of Northwold ceased operations with the four-vehicle fleet passing to H W Carter in nearby Foulden, together with most of the services. Others were covered by extensions or modifications to existing Towler routes. In October 1981, the Towler management retired; 5 of the coaches and the service commitments passed to Mrs L G Carter (widow of H W Carter) of Foulden. In turn, four of L G Carter's coaches passed to Coach Services of Thetford in February 1988 when the Carter operator's licence was revoked. Despite the combination of the operator's routes, twenty years later duplicates had faded into history! However the flats built on the bus-operating site in London Road are named Towlers Court.

Livery: cream and mid blue (Towler's)
cream and dark blue (F G Carter)

Reg	Chassis	Body	Seats	New	In	Ex	Out
F G Carter, Riverside, Northwold, Norfolk							
HL 5333	Leyland TD2	Roe	H26/22C	1932	5/48	West Riding (28)	5/50

Double-Deckers operated 1959 - 1967

A Towler & Sons:							
RC 4623	AEC Regent	Willowbrook	L27/28R	1937	10/59	Trent (1341)	5/64
GWX 115	Bristol K6B	ECW	H30/26RD	1948	1/62	York-West Yorkshire (YDB68)	3/65
LUC 5	AEC Regent III	Park Royal	H30/26RD	1950	11/63	London Transport (RT1925)	6/67

Note - RC 4623 was originally fitted with a Weymann H28/26F body, the Willowbrook body was fitted in 1949

RC 4623 (above)
A well-laden double-decker, resplendent in blue and cream, waits for time on Angel Hill, Bury St Edmunds, in June 1961 before returning home to Brandon via the Thetford Forest. Alongside is a 1957 Commer Avenger III/Plaxton (LRJ 866) of Carter's, Northwold, about to make a similar journey.

G R Mills

GWX 115 (below)
Highbridge Bristol K/ECW double-deckers were a familiar sight in East Anglia as Eastern Counties operated examples on city services in Cambridge, Norwich and Peterborough, but very few strayed into the independent sector. The Towler bus had previously worked in York city. The damage to the roof dome from the Norfolk and Suffolk trees is obvious in this August 1963 view at the depot.

G R Mills

Phoenix Student Travel Ltd, Bates Road, Maldon, Essex

Phoenix was originally set up by Bob Farrell in February 2000 to administer school contract services provided by First Eastern National and First Thamesway. The initial fleet was operated on Essex Buses licences, legal lettering, servicing and a dedicated rota of drivers on spreadover duties. Vehicles were outstationed at Braintree, Basildon and Chelmsford First bus depots as well as Ensign's Purfleet premises. A block tender submitted to the Anglo-European school at Ingatestone resulted in 11 routes operating through the village. Combined with services to 12 other schools, the distinctive buses were seen throughout the Colchester, Chelmsford and Southend area.

Increased fleet requirements were met with ex London Leyland Olympians rapidly converted to single-door by Ensign, such that several entered service in red livery but met the Essex CC requirement that precludes the use of dual-door buses on school contracts. Prior to the granting of Phoenix own operators licence in April 2002, all the 6xxx numbered Olympians displayed Ensign psv discs. As the vehicles were always idle at weekends, they were ideal for rail replacement work when planned maintenance on the track occurred. Similarly during school holidays, spare drivers were available which led to the acquisition of an ex-Colchester Atlantean that had been converted to open-top by Guide Friday for use at Portsmouth. Repainted into City Sightseeing red to provide the Colchester tour for the 2003 season, in the event the bus was only used for a very short period before a mechanical failure put it off the road. Replaced on some weekends by an Ensign generic open-topper, the regular performer became a standard "school bus" without commentary with disastrous results on any potential patronage.

The company ceased abruptly in October 2003 causing considerable distress to parents who had paid for season tickets. Stephensons of Rochford took over the operating centre, albeit reduced in size, together with some of the vehicles, services and staff. The acquired buses were all gradually repainted white and pale green to operate:

501	Chelmsford - Billericay - Southend
503	Althorne - Southminster - South Woodham - Southend
504	Wickham Bishops - Maldon - South Woodham - Southend
505	Great Baddow - Maldon - Colchester
510	Ostend - Southminster - North Fambridge - Chelmsford
513	Little Waltham - Chelmsford - East Hanningfield - Southend
514	Hatfield Peverel - Chelmer Village - South Woodham - Westcliff

None of the Anglo-European work was adopted by Stephensons, as Nelsons (NIBS) of Wickford and Fargo Coachlines of Rayne became the main contractors into Ingatestone.

Livery: purple with pink bands

Double-Deckers operated 2000 - 2003

	Reg	Chassis	Body	Seats	New	In	Ex	Out
Essex Buses								
5001	JTY 371X	Leyland ONLXB/1R	ECW	H45/32F	1981	9/00	Go North East (3611)	7/03
5002	JTY 382X	Leyland ONLXB/1R	ECW	H45/32F	1981	9/00	Go North East (3582)	7/03
5003	JTY 395X	Leyland ONLXB/1R	ECW	H45/32F	1981	9/00	Go North East (3595)	7/03
5004	JTY 400X	Leyland ONLXB/1R	ECW	H45/32F	1981	9/00	Go North East (3600)	7/03
5005	XWY 478X	Leyland ONLXB/1R	ECW	H45/32F	1982	9/00	Arriva Tees (203)	7/03
5006	SJR 616Y	Leyland ONLXB/1R	ECW	H45/32F	1983	9/00	Go North East (3616)	7/03
EnsignBus								
6000	C807 BYY	Leyland ONLXB/1R	ECW	H42/30F	1986	9/01	Selkent (L7)	10/03
6001	C811 BYY	Leyland ONLXB/1R	ECW	H42/30F	1986	9/01	Selkent (L11)	10/03
6002	C62 CHM	Leyland ONLXB/1R	ECW	H42/30F	1986	9/01	Selkent (L62)	10/03
6003	C64 CHM	Leyland ONLXB/1R	ECW	H42/30F	1986	9/01	Selkent (L64)	10/03
6004	C82 CHM	Leyland ONLXB/1R	ECW	H42/30F	1986	9/01	Selkent (L82)	10/03
6005	C86 CHM	Leyland ONLXB/1R	ECW	H42/30F	1986	9/01	Selkent (L86)	10/03
6006	C92 CHM	Leyland ONLXB/1R	ECW	H42/30F	1986	9/01	Selkent (L92)	10/03
6007	C77 CHM	Leyland ONLXB/1R	ECW	H42/30F	1986	9/01	Selkent (L77)	10/03
6008	C94 CHM	Leyland ONLXB/1R	ECW	H42/30F	1986	9/01	Selkent (L94)	10/03
6009	C109 CHM	Leyland ONLXB/1R	ECW	H42/30F	1986	9/01	Selkent (L109)	10/03
6010	C110 CHM	Leyland ONLXB/1R	ECW	H42/30F	1986	9/01	Selkent (L110)	10/03
6011	C106 CHM	Leyland ONLXB/1R	ECW	H42/30F	1986	9/01	Selkent (L109)	10/03
6012	C28 CHM	Leyland ONLXB/1R	ECW	H42/30F	1986	9/01	Selkent (L28)	10/03
6013	B204 DTU	Leyland ONLXB/1R	ECW	H42/27F	1985	9/01	Arriva Midlands North (1924)	10/01
6014	C44 CHM	Leyland ONLXB/1R	ECW	H42/30F	1986	9/02	Selkent (L44)	10/03
6015	C81 CHM	Leyland ONLXB/1R	ECW	H42/30F	1986	9/02	Selkent (L81)	10/03
6016	C818 BYY	Leyland ONLXB/1R	ECW	H42/30F	1986	9/02	Selkent (L18)	10/03

Reg	Chassis	Body	Seats	New	In	Ex	Out
6017	C54 CHM	Leyland ONLXB/1R	ECW	H42/30F	1986	9/02	Selkent (L54)	10/03
6018	C91 CHM	Leyland ONLXB/1R	ECW	H42/30F	1986	9/02	Selkent (L91)	10/03
6019	C108 CHM	Leyland ONLXB/1R	ECW	H42/30F	1986	9/02	Selkent (L108)	10/03
6020	C104 CHM	Leyland ONLXB/1R	ECW	H42/30F	1986	9/02	Selkent (L104)	10/03
7000	YNO 77S	Leyland AN68/1R	ECW	O43/31F	1978	10/02	Guide Friday, Stratford-u-Avon	10/03
	C668 LJR	Leyland ONCL10/1RV	ECW	H40/30F	1985	7/03	Go Northern (3668)	10/03
	CBV 2S	Bristol VRT/SL3/BLXB	ECW	O43/31F	1977	5/03	Mercury Radio (non psv)	10/03
	C112 CAT	Dennnis Dominator	East Lancs H43/28F	1986	2/03	Northern Blue, Burnley	10/03

Notes:
CBV 2S and C112 CAT were not operated
XWY 478X was new to West Riding (478)
B504 DTU was new to Crosville (EOG204) and was a short term loan from Ensign
YNO 77S was new to Colchester (77)

CBV 2S was new to Ribble (2002) with a Leyland 501 engine
C112 CAT was new to Kingston-upon-Hull (112)
6000-12/14-20 were new to London Transport
6018 was previously registered WLT 491 and was reregistered to C507 OTW

5003: JTY 395X (left)
Typifying the first batch of six Olympians with a full set of vinyls including fleetnames, First logos and the light blue phoenix on the rear side panels, 5003 is seen on a Sunday rail replacement working in January 2002 at Witham station. The contract for buses during the planned permanent way maintenance had been awarded to FirstBus on that occasion.

G R Mills

CBV 2S (right)
Originally one of a batch of 20 new to Ribble with Leyland 501 engines in July 1977, CBV 2S was transferred within the Stagecoach group to Cumberland and converted to open-top to work on the Ambleside - Bowness-on-Windermere "Lakeland experience" service. Seen at Bates Road, Maldon, prior to repaint into Phoenix livery.

G R Mills

6000: C807 BYY (right)
Numerically the first of 14 Olympians provided by Ensignbus for the new school year in 2001, 6000 is returning to the Maldon base in May 2003 having worked route 515 to Westcliff. The second wave of Olympians did not receive the phoenix over the rear side panels and windows.

G R Mills

Theobalds Coaches Ltd, Station Yard, Long Melford, Suffolk

During the early post-war years, despite the buoyant stage services and excursion operations, Theobalds vehicle intake was confined to new and used Bedford OB models. The fleet was operated from a small workshop approached via a passage at the side of the company's cyclist/motorist shop, which was also able to sell petrol. As the fleet grew in numbers, a small garage was built on the opposite side of Little St Mary's, the main street through Long Melford, again with a narrow approach between cottages. An outstation was also used at the Old Fire Station, The Green, Hartest, where a shop selling radios and motoring accessories, with a hand-operated petrol pump alongside, had been acquired from J W Cook, together with a Bean bus and service licences, in 1933.

On 10 August 1959, Corona Coaches Ltd of Sudbury went into liquidation and all operations ceased. Theobalds were awarded all the former Long, Glemsford, services which Corona had only gained 12 months earlier. Additional petrol-engined Bedford coaches were promptly purchased but the most significant intake was the first ever double-deckers which were also the first diesel-engined buses in the fleet. An additional double-decker was required when Theobalds gained a group of routes serving Sudbury, formerly provided by Goldsmiths of Sicklesmere. Parking accommodation for the expanding fleet was provided by demolishing a group of cottages opposite the office/shop and creating a concrete hardstanding area for eight buses.

In 1982, the company moved into a purpose-built office and garage building in the goods yard area of the disused Long Melford Station, which had been on the lines from Sudbury to Bury St Edmunds (closed in April 1961) and Haverhill (closed 6 March 1967). Both these closures had an effect on the double-deck operation: Firstly, the notorious low bridge crossing the A134 main road through Long Melford was removed allowing high bridge type double-deckers unhindered passage. Secondly, the link to Haverhill was provided by an express service operated by Theobalds to connect with Eastern Counties service 113 to Cambridge. From January 1971 this service was converted to normal stage operation and double-deckers were frequently used.

By March 1990, the business had been put up for sale by tender but no firm buyer was declared. An offer from Partridge & Son was due to take effect on 21 December 1990 but this was not finalised. In the following April, receivers were called in to dispose of the assets. Roy Munson, proprietor of Beeston's, Hadleigh, and Mulley's Motorways, Ixworth, made a successful bid for almost the entire fleet, the work commitments and the property. Operations continued from the Long Melford site as a sub-depot of Beeston's until August 2000 when the property was sold to developers for the erection of a new, maltings-style, block of flats conforming with the converted maltings already in-situ. The original office/workshop passed to an antiques dealer and later an estate agent, while the parking area and garage site became the Long Melford fire station. The outstation at Hartest reverted to a traditional village garage, still with old style petrol pumps at the roadside, but ceased to serve fuel when the self-service era dawned.

Livery: green and cream

Double-Deckers operated 1959 - 1991

Reg	Chassis	Body	Seats	New	In	Ex	Out
BDR 269	Leyland TD5	Leyland	L27/28R	1939	11/59	Lansdowne, London E11	3/66
ADR 813	Leyland TD5	Leyland	L27/28R	1938	12/59	Lansdowne, London E11	10/64
MWL 987	AEC Regent III	NCB	L27/26R	1948	7/61	City of Oxford (L353)	7/67
OFC 379	AEC Regent III	Park Royal	L26/26R	1950	10/64	City of Oxford (L155)	9/70
CDJ 879	Leyland PD2/10	Davies	H30/26R	1954	3/66	St Helens (79)	3/72
XGB 779	Leyland PD2/30	Alexander	H31/28R	1959	9/68	Smith, Barrhead	9/75
LJX 16	AEC Regent V	Metro-Cammell	H40/32F	1959	9/70	Halifax (16)	4/78
LJX 18	AEC Regent V	Metro-Cammell	H40/32F	1959	6/74	Green Bus, Rugeley	3/77
PFN 864	AEC Regent V	Park Royal	FH40/32F	1958	9/74	Crusader, Harlow	9/79
DAU 379C	AEC Renown	Weymann	H40/30F	1965	9/76	Nottingham (379)	9/88
DAU 364C	AEC Renown	Weymann	H40/30F	1965	3/77	Nottingham (364)	1/87
JKE 336E	Leyland PDR1/1	Massey	H43/31F	1967	3/77	Maidstone (36)	4/91
65 RTO	Daimler CRG6LX	NCME	H43/33F	1963	12/77	Nottingham (65)	5/86
JKE 338E	Leyland PDR1/1	Massey	H43/31F	1967	5/78	Maidstone (38)	4/91
ABN 201B	Leyland PDR1/1	East Lancs	H45/33F	1964	4/79	Hedingham Omnibuses (L90)	1/88
JKE 337E	Leyland PDR1/1	Massey	H43/31F	1967	9/82	Lodge, High Easter	8/89
PRG 131J	Daimler CRG6LX-33	Alexander	H48/32D	1971	8/84	Partridge, Hadleigh	4/91
JKE 341E	Leyland PDR1/1	Massey	H43/31F	1967	5/86	Osborne's, Tollesbury (1)	12/87
WBN 966L	Leyland AN68/1R	Park Royal	H43/32F	1972	11/87	GM Buses (7088)	4/91
PRG 135J	Daimler CRG6LX-33	Alexander	H48/32D	1971	1/88	Partridge, Hadleigh	4/91
JGA 206N	Leyland AN68/1R	Alexander	H45/31F	1975	8/89	Partridge, Hadleigh	4/91

Notes:
ADR 813 and BDR 269 were new to Plymouth (213/32) with
Weymann L24/24R bodies, the Leyland L27/28R bodies were
fitted in 1953 and the buses were renumbered 141/7
LJX 18 was new to Halifax (18)
PFN 864 was new to East Kent

ABN 201B was new to Bolton (201)
JKE 337E and JKE 341E were new to Maidstone (37, 41)
PRG 131/5J were new to Aberdeen (later Grampian), (131/5)
JGA 206N was new to Glasgow (LA927)

(Ref: *Buses Extra 73*, October/November 1991)

ADR 813 and BDR 269 (top right)
The only pre-war chassis to be rebodied by Leyland were eight
TD5s for Plymouth; two of which were acquired by Theobalds to
cover ex-Corona work. The pair is seen at rest in Long Melford in
September 1962.

G R Mills

LJX 18 and LJX 16 (second from top right)
The removal of the railway bridge in Long Melford enabled
Theobalds to buy highbridge double-deckers and the first
front-entrance models in the fleet appear particularly tall in this
January 1975 view of the two ex-Halifax Regent Vs on the garage
forecourt.

G R Mills

DAU 364C and DAU 379C (bottom right)
These two were from a rare batch of 35 AEC Renowns with
full-height Metro Cammell bodies new to Nottingham. Note the
pole strengthener between the bonnet and the upper deck. 379
was later converted to open-top and was operated by Norfolk,
Nayland; Hedingham Omnibuses and Partridges of Hadleigh.

G R Mills

PRG 135J and PRG 131J (top left)
Seen at Sudbury Upper School in November 1990 this pair
of former Aberdeen Fleetlines was acquired from Partridges.
135 has the final flamboyant livery adopted while 131 is in the
traditional pre-1986 style.

G R Mills

JKE 338-336E (bottom)
Massey bodied Atlanteans were rare outside the boroughs of
Colchester and Maidstone. Theobalds bought a pair of the latter
via Ensignbus (336/8) and filled in "the gap" with 337 from Lodges
of High Easter. The trio are lined up by the old Watneys brewery
(later converted to flats) in the old Long Melford Station yard in
May 1984.

G R Mills

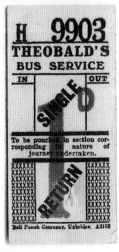

A H Wells, Glebefield Road, Hatfield Peverel, Essex
A H Wells, The Garage, Wantz Road, Maldon, Essex from 1967

This psv business was initially a partnership between V Sorrell and A H "Bob" Wells, with the vehicles parked in a yard in Spring Lane, Witham, prior to a move to part of the Wayside Café in Hatfield Peverel. Bob, who had been in the garage business, went as a sole proprietor in March 1961, with a Ford/Burlingham coach. He took over the jointly owned Ford/Duple five months later. The subsequent additions to the fleet were a cosmopolitan selection including a Crossley/Duple that had been rebuilt to full-front, a Morris Commercial/Wadham and a pair of Daimler Freelines. However, Ford models were favoured for most new and many used coaches over subsequent years.

The need for double-deckers arose when Crompton Parkinson relocated from Chelmsford to Witham and the factory workforce required transport to the new site. Some unexpected weekend work was gained during November and December in 1967 due to a prolonged strike by Southend Transport road staff. Earlier the same year, the six-coach fleet of L Hall & Sons, Queen Street, Maldon (established in August 1920) was acquired. The garage and workshop remained in Hall's ownership and the pantechnicons continued to operate from the site. Eventually a set of lock up car garages were demolished adjacent to the garage and the entire Wells fleet was transferred to the new premises, which, with a new exit from the site involved a change of address whilst the garage remained in the same position!

Bob retired to his home, named "Chara" at Wickham Bishops in October 1984 and sold his 13-coach fleet to Tony Ford of Althorne who continued to have vehicles based at the Maldon premises until the expiry of the lease in 1988. The garage was subsequently demolished and the developed for housing. Similarly, a block of flats had by then replaced the café yard at Hatfield Peverel.

Livery: white and red

Double-Deckers operated 1965 - 1970

Reg	Chassis	Body	Seats	New	In	Ex	Out
KNG 371	Bristol K5G	ECW	L27/26R	1949	10/65	Eastern Counties (LK371)	11/67
LOU 38	Dennis Lance K4	East Lancs	L28/28R	1954	2/66	Aldershot & District (210)	10/68
GTY 170	Leyland PD2/12	Met-Camm	H32/28R	1954	10/66	Tyneside (40)	10/70

LOU 38 (above)
Originally part of a batch of 32 Dennis Lance K4 (with 5LW engines) delivered to Aldershot & District in 1953/54. Twelve were bodied by Weymann but the Wells example was one of the 20 with a better styled East Lancs body. LOU 38 is seen at the Wayside Café at Hatfield Peverel in May 1967 in company with a 1949 Austin CXD/Mann Egerton newly acquired from the Hall of Maldon fleet.

G R Mills

GTY 170 (below)
Binns shops are unknown in the south of England, so when the Wells PD2 was seen in the Chelmsford and Maldon areas, unchanged from its days in Gateshead in olive green and white and a local advert on the front panel, it was dubbed "Bobs Binns bus". Caught at work turning at Newington Avenue, on route 6 during the Southend Transport strike in November 1967.

G R Mills

G H N Whybrow (t/a Kelvedon Coaches), 215 High Street, Kelvedon, Essex

Geoff first entered into psv operation with an 11-seat minibus in August 1965. Four years later, the fleet had enlarged to three Bedford OBs and a pair of minibuses operated from Clark's Farm in Cranes Lane, Kelvedon. Double-deck operation was tried for the start of the 1972 school year but the vehicle was sold during the Christmas holidays. Although the Guy was a characteristic traditional half-cab, the curious 12 volt electrical system and the open rear platform, and thus the need for crew operation, meant that the bus was not very commercially practical, especially as AEC Bridgemasters and Dennis Lolines with front-entrance bodywork were available on the second-hand market. Operators such as Osborne's of Tollesbury, with a daily service through Kelvedon, already had a pair of Bridgemasters and the more modern Renown.

When National Travel (South East) was disbanded as the coach fleet returned to Eastern National in October 1978, the ex-Moore Bros office, garage and yard became vacant. Geoff bravely leased the workshop and the rearmost yard enabling his fleet to move from a rented portion of a road resurfacing contractor's yard in Maldon Road to the large High Street site. To offset the increased costs, a large number of ex-London DMSs were prepared for MoTs prior to shipment to Hong Kong by Ensignbus.

The close association with the renowned dealer led to some interesting rolling stock being introduced for additional school contracts - a trio of Leyland Panthers with dual door Marshall bodies new to Exeter, were acquired for the new school year in September 1981. Unfortunately the business was forced to cease trading in March 1983 and the 14-vehicle fleet was auctioned off. Regrettably the pair of Fleetlines and the Atlantean did not see any further psv service. The latter, which had been decapitated under a low bridge in Rivenhall End, passed to Harwich & Dovercourt Coaches who planned to put it to use for tree pruning and possible certification for weddings and carnivals, but in the event this did not materialise.

Livery: maroon and white

Double-Deckers operated 1972 - 1983

Reg	Chassis	Body	Seats	New	In	Ex	Out
883 DTB	Guy Arab IV	NCME	H41/32R	1957	9/72	Ford, Althorne	12/72
DAU 432C	Leyland PDR1/2	Met-Camm	H44/33F	1965	5/81	Davies, Rye	3/83
BCS 968C	Daimler CRG6LX	Alexander	H44/31F	1965	9/82	G & G, Wickford	3/83
BCS 984C	Daimler CRG6LX	Alexander	H44/31F	1965	9/82	G & G, Wickford	3/83

Notes:
883 DTB was new to Lancashire United (616)
DAU 432C was new to Nottingham (432)

BCS 968/84C were new to Western SMT (R1985, R2001)

DAU 432C (above)
This Atlantean came to Essex in pale blue livery but is seen in Cranes Lane, Kelvedon, in August 1981 fully repainted into white with two maroon bands. The front near side panel has the word "Schools" signwritten on, as this was before the advent of the obligatory yellow signs with the silhouette of two walking children.
G R Mills

BCS 968C (below)
One of a pair of Fleetlines acquired via Ensign in an all over navy blue livery; seen in December 1982 after a full repaint into white and maroon returning to Kelvedon along the old London Road. The A12 trunk road can be seen across the background (left to right).
G R Mills

Wiffens Coaches Ltd, Sunnyside, Finchingfield, Essex

The family pioneered a service into Braintree operating on Mondays, Wednesdays, Fridays and Saturdays in pre-war years, but the licence was relinquished after the war as patronage moved away to a rival facility via an alternative route provided by Eastern National. However a Tuesday, Friday and Saturday service into Saffron Walden survived the passage of time.

The first new post-war coaches were the famed Bedford OB/Duple Vista C29F combination, the fifth example being graced with a "777" registration. By 1980 the fleet had included eleven new coaches with same individual numbers, but the choice of chassis had swung away from General Motors products to Ford Motor Co models.

A venture into dedicated school buses in 1973 introduced double-deck operation, and these formed part of the fleet consistently until 1987. By that time, Wiffens had established a programme of quality holiday tours provided by six Bova Futuras, four of which were new. These were serviced and maintained in a purpose built garage that was carefully designed to suit the undulating site and to be sympathetic with the landscape in what is probably the most picturesque village in Essex. A small office was set up at Stansted Airport to organise cabin crew flight transfers but the hoped for success in tendering for the car-park passenger shuttles never materialised.

The company reverted to dedicated school transport in 1989 with a set of one-time Edinburgh Bedford YRTs with rare Alexander Y-Type bodies but the contract fleet all passed to S Cook (t/a Flagfinders) of Braintree in September 1998. The operational site was sold for executive housing, appropriately named Coach Field, which again was of a discreet design appropriate to an area of exceptional charm.

Livery: duo-green and white

Double-Deckers operated 1964 - 1987

Reg	Chassis	Body	Seats	New	In	Ex	Out
GPW 356	Leyland PD1A	ECW	L27/26R	1947	5/64	Eastern Counties (AP356)	11/64
997 GHN	Bristol LD6B	ECW	H33/27RD	1958	4/73	United (132)	3/77
505 DKT	Leyland PDR1/1	Met-Camm	H44/33F	1958	1/76	Maidstone & District (5505)	11/79
NRN 574	Leyland PDR1/1	MCW	L39/33F	1659	10/76	Ribble (1574)	8/77
KBB 240D	Leyland PDR1/1	Alexander	H43/34F	1966	8/77	Tyne & Wear (240)	11/80
KBB 128D	Leyland PDR1/1	MCW	H44/34F	1966	11/79	Tyne & Wear (128)	11/81
BCS 959C	Daimler CRG6LX	Alexander	H44/31F	1965	11/80	Western SMT (1976)	12/80
MLK 677L	Daimler CRL6	Park Royal	H44/34F	1973	1/81	London Transport (DMS677)	9/87
KJD 94P	Daimler CRL6	Park Royal	H45/33F	1976	12/81	London Transport (DMS2094)	9/87

997 GHN (left)

The first Lodekkas released by NBC subsidiaries onto the open market were the Bristol engined models, the more economical Gardner powered stock being retained. The Wiffen example complete with Cave-Brown-Cave heating intakes, resplendent in duo-green with white bands rests at Rayne Station in December 1974.

G R Mills

KBB 240D (right)

From 1976 to 1981 the Atlantean was the preferred choice, with a pair in stock throughout this period. This example replaced a lowheight "basic box" style Metro-Cammell that had a short life with Wiffens and is seen at Rayne Station on layover between schools in July 1980.

G R Mills

P E K Baldwin, White House, Waterloo, Beccles, Suffolk

Initially commencing as a minibus operator in 1969, using the fleetname Wangford Minibus Hire, the introduction of full size coaches in 1979 prompted the use of Waterloo Coaches as a more appropriate fleetname. Interestingly, the pair of Duple bodied Bedford VAMs that pioneered the upgrade were both ex-Stockdale (t/a Nightingale) of Beccles when that operation ceased in October 1979. B R Shreeve of Lowestoft had owned the latter business from 1942 to 1951 and three of the final fleet went to Shreeve's Belle Coaches operation. In 1984, Baldwin moved to the Ellough Industrial Estate at Beccles, an area which was also home to Lamberts Coaches and Wayland Minibus, and there was a later move to Thurton in Norfolk. After Master Travel of Norwich ceased operations in January 1991, the fleetname was adopted by Baldwin, who ceased trading in July 1992.

Livery: cream and red

Reg	Chassis	Body	Seats	New	In	Ex	Out
BHL 609K	Daimler CRG6LX	NCME	H43/33F	1972	4/91	Rodemark, Herstmonceux	1/92

Note - BHL 609K was new to West Riding (709)

BHL 609K
Originally one of 25 Daimler Fleetlines supplied to West Riding in 1972, the bus was with Autopoint in East Sussex before service in Norfolk, and went on to Porteous (t/a Alpha and Grey de-Luxe) of Hull. Note the non standard appearance of the upper deck front corner panels in this view unloading school children in Bracondale, Norwich in October 1991.

G R Mills

D W Fosdike (t/a Advance Coaches), Waterloo Mill, Bramfield, Suffolk

David Fosdike started in the coaching business in April 1961 with a 1948 Foden/Plaxton ½ cab. Two years later an underfloor-engined Seddon/Duple C41C was added which had been new to the famous Ted Heath band. New Ford/Plaxton coaches were purchased in 1967/73/5/6/8 and a new Volvo/Plaxton was added in 1981. When C E Naylor, of Angel Yard, Halesworth retired in November 1971 from a business established in the mid 1920's, David Fosdike acquired four coaches and the double-decker, all of which were withdrawn within a year, and stage services from Halesworth to Harleston, Lowestoft, Beccles and Cratfield. Fosdike later acquired a pair of Bristol LS/ECW which had been secondhand to Eastern Counties, and a pair of AEC Swift/ECW when the Waveney fleet at Lowestoft ceased operations. The final coach, a Plaxton bodied Quest VM ex-Excelsior of Bournemouth went on to two further Suffolk operators after Fosdike ceased operations in June 1988; the work and four Ford coaches passed to Howes of Halesworth.

Livery: cream and maroon

Reg	Chassis	Body	Seats	New	In	Ex	Out
WJO 183	AEC Regent V	Park Royal	L30/26RD	1955	11/71	Naylor, Halesworth	11/72

Note - WJO 183 was new to City of Oxford (183)

WJO 183
Retaining Naylor's duo-blue livery (the firm once traded as Halesworth Blue Bus Services), the 20 year old double-decker, an unusual exposed radiator Regent V once a member of the fine City of Oxford fleet, has come to an undignified end as this view in a soggy Halesworth field in March 1975 sadly shows.

G R Mills

A M Goodwin, London Road, Black Notley, Essex

Alan had been a full time driver with Wells of Hatfield Peverel and later Boons of Boreham before going it alone in March 1973. Initially the intake had a Bedford bias but a pair of Bristol LHLs and later an LHS broke the mould. However it was for the ex-Boon Seddon Pennine VI that Alan was best known, as it was kept in superb order and rallied for many years in the eighties. The need for a double-decker arose when numbers increased beyond a coach capacity on the school run from Stebbing to the Helena Romanes School in Great Dunmow, which was operated for 26 years. The double-decker was sold after 3 years to a nightclub owner in Lowestoft, only to be burnt out in an arson attack. Alan ceased operations in May 2006 and the two remaining coaches passed to Wicks of Braintree, together with the yard which had been leased from Wicks.

Livery: silver-grey and blue

Reg	Chassis	Body	Seats	New	In	Ex	Out
TET 748S	Daimler CRL6	Roe	H43/33F	1977	1/00	Dons, Dunmow	3/03

Note - TET 748S was new to Samuel Morgan (Reliance), Stainforth, later South Yorkshire PTE (1129)

TET 748S
Smartly attired in white and blue, with a silver-grey band, the Daimler Fleetline/Roe is seen in Little Waltham village in June 2000 bound for the North Weald Bus Rally on hire to the Colchester meeting of the PSV Circle. The ex-South Yorkshire PTE destination blind shows "Worksop".

G R Mills

C E Halls, The Stag Inn, Hatfield Heath, Essex

The earliest vehicles on the Stag Bus Service into Bishops Stortford were a 1933 Bedford WLB and a 1947 Bedford OB. Both were new to Halls and had bodywork by Thurgood of Ware, built only 20 miles away. Two further locally bodied Bedfords were acquired second-hand on WTB chassis, via Thurgoods acting as dealers. From 1952 to 1980, Bedford was the favoured choice with a variety of Duple bodied models being acquired, all of which were preowned stock. Operations passed to Frank D Hornsby of Little Canfield in October 1986 and then to Ray P Vidler, Railway Sidings, Henham in September 1998. The business finally closed in August 2003.

Livery: light blue and cream

Reg	Chassis	Body	Seats	New	In	Ex	Out
DNH 197	Daimler CVD6	Roe/Park Royal	H30/26R	1953	10/69	Northampton (197)	12/75

Note - DNH 197 passed into preservation

DNH 197
The only double-decker to grace Halls fleet was this classic Daimler with smart chrome radiator as seen at the Downfield House yard in January 1970. The bus retained the original Northampton red livery which was ideal when it was purchased by the late Richard Brewis of Borley, Essex, for preservation.

G R Mills

P & M Coach Line Ltd, Portman Road, Ipswich, Suffolk

This fleet was formed in 1939 by the amalgamation of S J Raymer (t/a Primrose Coaches) and C R Nugent (t/a Marguerite Coaches), initially with a fleet of Gilfords. A pair of Leyland TD1s were acquired in 1942 but these were not operated as double-deckers as they were cut down to single-deck and rebuilt by Archer to C32F. A similar exercise was performed on an AEC Regent in 1947 prior to the delivery of a new Maudslay/Whitson. This was followed by a Maudslay/Plaxton, a pair of AEC Regal IIIs with Plaxton bodies and a luxurious pair of Maudslay/Plaxton with full front coachwork and low seating capacity. The company built up a reputation for quality tours in the 50s and 60s. The unique Sentinel-Beadle was acquired from Southern National in June 1960 to operate the Ipswich to Otley route acquired from Turners Bus service in August 1950. P & M came under the control of Harris (International Progressive Coachline) of Cambridge during the 1960s and a double-decker was transferred from the parent company to work a contract to the BX Plastics Factory at Brantham near Manningtree. However when P & M went into receivership in 1968 the bus and the contract passed to Partridge of Hadleigh, Suffolk.

Livery: duo-blue

Reg	Chassis	Body	Seats	New	In	Ex	Out
NEH 453	Leyland OPD2/1	NCME	L27/26RD	1949	3/66	Potteries (L453)	11/68

NEH 453

This hybrid Leyland OPD2/1 was new with a Weymann B35F; in 1954 it received the body shown, which had been removed from a 1936 Leyland TD5 (DVT 901). After arrival in Cambridgeshire, the bus was repainted into white with green Progressive livery but on transfer to P & M received the duo-blue paintwork as seen in Constantine Road, Ipswich, in February 1969.

G R Mills

N A Read (t/a Ferrers Coaches), Hullbridge Road, South Woodham, Essex

Norman entered psv ownership with the acquisition from Emberson of South Woodham of a pair of 1936 Thurgood bodied Dodges, which had been new to Our Bus Service, Grays. The latter business was taken over by Eastern National on 15 September 1951 only to pass to London Transport (Country Area) two weeks later! Read had a variety of stock, including a Leyland Comet/Devon Coach Builders, a Daimler CVD6 with a secondhand Whitson body transferred from a Leyland TS2; a Foden/Bellhouse-Hartwell and three 3-cylinder Trojans. The ever-popular Bedfords were followed by a strong Ford bias in the 70s and 80s. Following the death of Norman Read, his son Geoffrey and grandson Anthony formed Ferrers Coaches Ltd in 1985 which ceased operations in January 2000.

Livery: duo-blue

Reg	Chassis	Body	Seats	New	In	Ex	Out
ADR 814	Leyland TD5	Leyland	L27/28R	1938	9/60	Plymouth (144)	3/62

Note - ADR 814 was new to Plymouth (214) with a Weymann L24/24R body, the Leyland body was fitted 1953 (as 144)

ADR 814

Originally one of eight Leyland TD5s that were rebodied for Plymouth, this example was outlived by the similar pair at Theobalds, Long Melford. Fully repainted into the duo-blue Ferrers Coaches livery, the bus is shown at the depot yard in July 1961.

G R Mills

Rules Coaches, Riverside, Boxford, Suffolk

With a history extending back to the twenties, this operator had established five service routes into Sudbury and two into Bury St Edmunds by the 1950s. Both new and second-hand Bedfords dominated the fleet from the 1930s through to the late '60s. Notable exceptions were a new AEC Regal III/Plaxton, the first diesel in the fleet, and the double-decker (the second diesel), which ironically had a body, built in the same year as the coach. A F Rule, the second generation of the family, was a skilled engineer and fitted diesel engines in many of the Bedford coaches. From 1968 to 1980, AEC Reliances formed the main intake. A very successful tours programme in the UK and abroad was operated for many years, latterly with a Van Hool bodied Volvo B10M. The stage services were gradually withdrawn as patronage declined, one of the last being a service into Colchester which started in June 1973 and ran until February 2000. The company ceased in March 2000 and the operating centre was sold for housing, appropriately named "Rules Yard".

RC 4639
Not requiring a repaint from Trent red and cream, the addition of fleetnames and a local destination blind customised the AEC Regent into the Rules fleet. The bus is seen at the Riverside garage yard in July 1961, home to the operations for over 70 years.

G R Mills

Livery: duo-red and cream

Reg	Chassis	Body	Seats	New	In	Ex	Out
RC 4639	AEC Regent	Willowbrook	L27/28R	1937	4/60	Trent (1346)	10/65

Note - RC 4639 was originally fitted with a Weymann H28/26F body, the Willowbrook body was fitted in 1949

P D & G Smith (t/a Smith Bros), 32 Centre Drive, Newmarket, Suffolk

This small enterprise ventured into the private hire market in April 1959 with a Commer Avenger with Whitson coachwork that was new to Saffords, Little Gransden, Cambridgeshire, operators of no less than 9 Commers between 1949 and 1968. Another Commer was later acquired, which, together with three Bedford SBs, passed to Mrs F A Carter of Bury Road, Kentford, Suffolk in March 1963. The latter business passed to Miller Bros, of Foxton in July 1965. Ironically, when the three Miller brothers set up their own individual businesses, John Miller established Mil-Ken Coaches a short hop from the former Carter garage in July 1965.

Livery: brown and cream

Reg	Chassis	Body	Seats	New	In	Ex	Out
BCK 940	Leyland PD1	Leyland	L27/26R	1947	8/60	Preston (107)	10/62
BUF 233	Leyland TD4	East Lancs	H28/24R	1935	9/62	Southdown (123)	3/63

Notes:
BCK 940 passed to the contractors Wiggins of Thundersley, Essex, for staff transport

BUF 233 was new with a Short H26/24R body, the East Lancs body was fitted in 1946, and went on approval to Norfolk's of Nayland but was not purchased

BCK 940
Seen in Newmarket Railway Station forecourt in October 1961 while on hire to Eastern Counties in the days when a fleet of double-deckers was required to take hordes of punters to the famed racecourse for the Cambridgeshire and Cesarewitch events. Alongside is an ex-Devon General AEC Regent III/Weymann operating for Palmer of Fordham (t/a Fordham & District) on the same duty.

G R Mills

G L Sutton, 54 Pier Avenue, Clacton-on-Sea, Essex

For many years, the company traded as Sutton's Crossley Coaches as the initial fleet included some Crossley X chassis with charabanc bodies by Munnions of Great Baddow. In the thirties, Sutton's became well known in the metropolis with a pair of TSMs fitted with well appointed observation style C31C coachwork by Strachans, lettered "Daily services London to Clacton-on-Sea". This practice continued through the post-war years on all the half cabs (AEC, Leyland and Maudslay chassis) and underfloor-engined coaches (AEC Reliances and Leyland Royal Tigers) acquired new between 1946 and 1960. In October 1967, Sutton's joined the Essex Coast Express pool with Eastern National and Grey-Green, but after six seasons sold their share to the latter. By this time, the fleet was 100% Ford, all bar one being second-hand, but as the company had ventured into school contracts, the rolling stock suited the task! Introduction of the double-decker improved the fleet content but unfortunately the business closed in September 1979. The head office and garage in Pier Avenue became a Boot's store.
Ref: Buses Extra 5: 1978
Livery: deep red and cream

Reg	Chassis	Body	Seats	New	In	Ex	Out
80 TVX	Bristol FLF6G	ECW	H38/32F	1960	1/78	Eastern National (2700)	9/79

80 TVX
Gleaming with sparkling bright red and cream replacing the previous NBC green livery, 80 TVX is fresh out of the paintshop in January 1978. Sutton's first and only double-decker was also Eastern National's first FLF. Interestingly, Suttons trade plates were 80 VX. The bus went on to be the first double-decker in the fleet of Cedric's at Wivenhoe - a true pioneer.

G R Mills

P D Wright (t/a Pullman Travel), 6 Marriott Close, Heigham Street, Norwich, Norfolk

First appearing in Norwich in June 1973 as Four Wheels Transport, with a pair of Ford Transit minibuses, the fleet rapidly grew to full size coaches even to the extent of a new Bedford YMT/Van Hool-McArdle being delivered in 1979. In 1982 two new Plaxton bodied Leyland Tigers and a new Bedford YNT/Duple joined the fleet. The final additions were a pair of ex London Country AEC Reliance/Duples. During 1983 a London express service was operated from Norwich via Wymondham, Attleborough and Thetford to Earls Court, this was taken on by Chenery of Dickleburgh, when Wright's business ceased in September 1984.

Livery: maroon and white

Reg	Chassis	Body	Seats	New	In	Ex	Out
933 GTA	Leyland PDR1/1	Metro-Cammell	O44/31F	1961	5/82	Western National (933)	3/83

Note - 933 GTA was new to Devon General (DL933)

933 GTA
Seen on 15 May 1982, the first day out in the new owners bright yellow livery, preparing to act as a grandstand at a sports ground at Rackheath, Norfolk. The bus was originally one of nine convertible open-toppers operated by Devon General, the batch was named after "Sea Dogs" and worked on the Torbay Riviera, the Torquay/Paignton coastline in Devon.

G R Mills

Non-PSV double-decker operators

Contractor:
F W Shanks (1962) Ltd, Park Road, Hunstanton, Norfolk
In the 1950s and 1960s before the days of widespread car ownership, building contractors had buses to transport the work force to construction sites. Interestingly, Shanks also had a pair of ex-London Q class single-deckers (CGJ 193/202) in this period. A green and cream livery was used.

Holiday Camp:
Shangri-La Holiday Caravan Park (later Oaklands Holiday Village), Colchester Road, St Osyth, Essex
Through out the '60s, the camp operated a double-decker to Clacton Railway station which was particularly busy on summer Saturdays. Eastern National took the enterprise to the Eastern Traffic Area Court unsuccessfully claiming that the service was not free. The camp owned three ex-Brighton, Hove & District Bristol K5G/ECW double-deckers (CAP 207/30/7) and three ex-Plymouth Leylands; two of which are illustrated below. CAP 230 went back to PSV work with Catt & Swinn (Best Coaches) of Great Bromley. All the double-deckers ran in "as acquired" livery.

JX 8362, this 1942 Leyland TD7 with Roe L27/26R body was new to Hebble (172) and is seen in somewhat battered condition, awaiting its scrapyard fate at Attleborough in July 1962. The Dodge lorry had been similarly condemned to the cutting torch. *G R Mills*

DDR 415 this 1947 Leyland PD1 with Weymann L27/26R body was new tp Plymouth (215) and is seen here loading at the camp in July 1962   *G R Mills*

HJY 278 a 1953 all-Leyland PD2/12 with H30/26R body, new to Plymouth (378), was the final double-decker owned and is seen here at the camp in July 1969   *G R Mills*

School:
St Michael's School, Ingoldisthorpe, Norfolk
The headmaster was a Rev Peter Potts (an unfortunate choice by his parents to be P Potts among school boys!) and the school consistently operated double-deckers into Hunstanton in the sixties. In addition to those illustrated, there was an ex-London Transport STL an ex-Eastern Counties Bristol K5G and an ex-London Transport RTW. A green livery was used.

CVP 234 was a Daimler COG5 new to Birmingham (1134) in 1937 with Metro-Cammell H30/24R body which came to St Michael's from Laurie (Chieftain), Hamilton, and is seen in July 1962.   *G R Mills*

FXT 278, another ex-London Transport AEC Regent with LPTB H30/26R body was new in 1940 (RT103) and is seen in July 1962.   *G R Mills*